In Fine Form

The Canadian Book
of Form Poetry

edited by
Kate Braid
and Sandy Shreve

POLESTAR
An Imprint of Raincoast Books

Raincoast Books acknowledges the ongoing financial support of the Government of Canada
through The Canada Council for the Arts and the Book Publishing Industry Development
Program (BPIDP); and the Government of British Columbia through the BC Arts Council.

Text design: Teresa Bubela

LIBRARY AND ARCHIVES CANADA CATALOGUING IN PUBLICATION

    In fine form : the Canadian book of form poetry / [edited by] Kate Braid
and Sandy Shreve.

Includes bibliographical references and index.
ISBN 1-55192-777-2

    1. Canadian poetry (English)—20th century. 2. Canadian poetry
(English)—21st century. 3. Literary form. I. Braid, Kate, 1947- II.
Shreve, Sandy

PS8279.I49 2005   C811'.6   C2005-900621-8

LIBRARY OF CONGRESS CONTROL NUMBER: 2005901196

Raincoast Books
9050 Shaughnessy Street
Vancouver, British Columbia
Canada, V6P 6E5
www.raincoast.com

At Raincoast Books we are committed to protecting the environment and to the responsible
use of natural resources. We are acting on this commitment by working with suppliers and
printers to phase out our use of paper produced from ancient forests. This book is one step
towards that goal. It is printed on 100% ancient-forest-free paper (40% post-consumer
recycled), processed chlorine- and acid-free, and supplied by New Leaf paper. It is printed
with vegetable-based inks. For further information, visit our website at www.raincoast.com.
We are working with Markets Initiative (www.oldgrowthfree.com) on this project.

Printed in Canada by Transcontinental Printing
10 9 8 7 6 5 4 3 2 1

CONTENTS

COUPLET CONT.

EPIGRAM 60

FUGUE AND MADRIGAL 68

... AND MORE CONT.

PREFACE

Anna Akmatova, writing in an age of experimentation, chose classical metres — suggesting, as Joseph Brodsky points out, that "her raptures and revelations were no greater than those of her predecessors." Curious, the idea that formal verse is a leveler.

From my own experience, it is a liberator — like the nut cracker that frees the kernel from its prison. But that is not quite right. No analogy is ever quite right.

I had a sculptor friend who worked in clay until she felt she was getting too sloppy, whereupon she turned to marble because the medium itself imposed its own discipline. "Free verse" and "formal verse" might be substituted for her "clay" and "marble."

As readers, the variety and intricate patterns of formal verse surprise us. Sometimes, by not surprising us at all. Like Mozart, for instance, and rhyming verse: one anticipates the note or the rhyme and then, when it comes, it is a consummation. It was what we expected but *more than we expected*: a deep satisfaction.

Also as readers, formal verse can teach us how to read. Like dancing with a professional, we are given no option but to acknowledge the pattern, fall in and become a part of the art. By paying strict attention, form can even provide a poem with additional meaning. Listen to the stresses in a stressed poem and the meaning will become clear.

This much welcomed anthology shows us what Canadian poets from the sixteenth century to the present day have done with form. Poets and readers alike will be grateful. Form is part of our heritage — free verse, an upstart. Not an unwanted or untalented upstart, but a newcomer nevertheless.

P.K. Page
Victoria, 2004

INTRODUCTION

In any poet's poem the shape is half the meaning.
— Louis MacNeice

The Seeds

This book springs from three roots — curiosity, necessity and a love of rhyme, repetition, metre and rhythm.

But first — what is form? It's a question we will return to, but in short, it's structure. A form poem is one in which key details of composition, including rhyme, repetition, metre and rhythm, are accepted as givens. Often these affect the poem's shape on the page, so a formal poem can sometimes be recognized at a glance — the fourteen lines of a sonnet, the three lines of the haiku, the somersaulting lines in the pantoum.

By the 1990s, the two of us had been writing form poems for some time and were finding that when we assigned them as exercises in writing classes and workshops, student work shone. But it seemed a contradiction — shouldn't being asked to write within tight restrictions limit a poet's free expression?

And therein lies the delicious paradox of form poetry. Ask any parent — constraint can generate freedom. So too, in poetry. Just look at a child's delight in rhyme and (what seems to the reading parent) endless repetition that becomes almost chant-like. And it's a pleasure we never entirely lose, though we may become more sophisticated and more subtle in our taste.

T.S. Eliot wrote: "Every revolution in poetry is ... a return to common speech."[1] In the early 1900s many North American poets saw the language of formal poetry as too often staid and limiting, and instead embraced the

---

[1] Eliot, T.S., "The Music of Poetry," the third W.P. Ker Memorial Lecture, delivered at Glasgow University in 1942 and published by Glasgow University Press, 1942. From *On Poetry and Poets* by T.S. Eliot in Geddes, Gary. *20th Century Poetry & Poetics: 4th Edition*. Toronto: Oxford University Press, 1996, p. 817.

colloquial tone of free verse (sometimes called open form). By the 1950s free verse had become the norm, and the tendency since then has been to pooh-pooh the elements of form poetry (especially metre and rhyme) as being old-fashioned.

But in our own work we were finding that closed and open forms each had their own challenges and delights. To write free verse well still required understanding the craft of poetry, and there were times when subject matter or mood called for a closed form — the obsessiveness of a sestina, for example, or the thoughtful depths of the glosa, the second look of the palindrome. Closed forms in particular reminded us how poetry is rooted in sound — the sensuous pleasure of repetition, the music of rhyme. We felt there was not only room, but a need, for both.

In 2000 Kate was asked to teach a course on writing poetry in form, but couldn't find an anthology with Canadian content. In lamenting this lack, the two of us came up with the idea of doing the book ourselves. We knew that Canadian poets, historically, had written a great deal in given forms and that many contemporary poets continued to include form poems in their books. As well, in recent years, more of this work was finding its way into literary journals. We suspected there was a resurgence of interest in this area, and began searching for form poems, thinking to compile a small book to show off the high calibre of Canadian work. Keeping our eyes peeled for clues to form in titles, notes and visual cues, we checked the individual collections, anthologies and literary magazines on our shelves, and scoured the Canadian poetry section of the Vancouver Public Library. By the time we were finished, we'd set aside an astonishing 1,400-plus poems (and read countless more) dating from the 1800s (and in one case, the 1600s) to the present.

But, we wondered, what were we missing? If this many poems had been published, how many more wonderful poems were still languishing on poets' desks? With some concern that we were about to be flooded with limericks, we put out a limited call for submissions, hoping for perhaps 200 to 300 poems to fill the inevitable gaps in our research. Within weeks we were knee deep in high quality form poems; by the time they stopped arriving, we had almost 1,000. This was an abundance we had never, in our wildest dreams, expected.

We immediately noticed patterns that clearly marked this work as arising from a distinct geography and cultural mix: the easy incorporation of the French language; the frequency of poems related to weather and to physical work like farming and fishing, and the influence of poets on one another's work within and across generations. We tracked, for instance, whole traditions of poets responding to P.K. Page's glosas and to John Thompson's ghazals. We found F.R. Scott responding to E.J. Pratt ("Brébeuf and His Brethren"), Phyllis Webb incorporating Fred Wah into her ghazal, Maxianne Berger acknowledging Christian Bök through an acrostic — delightful conversations over time, a call-and-response within the Canadian poetic tradition.

When is a form ...?

In editing more than 2,300 poems down to 175 for this volume, the question very quickly arose, when is a form not a form? Many fine poems, like the following by Anne Wilkinson, echoed and tantalized. But what category should we put it in?

STILL LIFE [2]

I'd love this body more
If graved in rigid wood
It could not move;
I'd cut it fresh in pine;
The little knots
Would show where muscles grew,
The hollows shadow ovals
Into eyes,
The grain be quick to point
The vein, be tendon's clue;
I'd whittle hair
A solid armoured hood

---

2   *Heresies: The Complete Poems of Anne Wilkinson 1924-1961*, edited by Dean Irvine. Montreal: Signal Editions, an imprint of Véhicule Press, 2003, p. 60.

And nothing here profane,
Nor rend the wood
But bind my fluid form
To forest tree,
Be still and let its green blood
Enter me.

Back and forth we wrote notes to each other: Syllabic? Almost. Regular metre? Sort of. How about rhyme? Kind of. We kept looking.

... not a form?

When we decided to do this anthology we were interested not only in the traditional forms, but also in what contemporary poets were doing with those traditions — and it's clear from the number of variations we found or received that Canadian poets are actively experimenting, using form for inspiration and in the service of a better poem. This raised the question of how far we would watch poets bend the tradition before we called it "not form."

In the case of the sonnet, for instance, a mark of its durability is that it was the second-largest category of poem we received (second only to stanzas). The variations seemed endless; poets dubbed their versions "liberated," "slender," "loose," "stretched," "eclectically rhymed," "word," "anti" and "free verse" sonnets.

But early on we decided the label sonnet and fourteen lines were not enough to convince us a poem fit the form. Beyond that, however, it was impossible to lay down a one-size-fits-all rule. In the end, we accepted a poem as a sonnet if the poet retained a clear echo of, and link to, the tradition by using roughly fourteen lines along with one or more of the form's other elements (rhyme and/or metre, a semblance of argument or persuasion, a concluding couplet, and so on). What proved interesting was how cleverly some poets disguised their forms. For example, it took months of careful reading, and a tip from poet Stephanie Bolster, before we recognized Diana Brebner's seven-couplet poems as sonnets.

The ghazal was also a challenge. Most of the ghazals we received (and there were many) were in the free verse mode made popular by poets like John

Thompson in Canada and Adrienne Rich in the United States. To distinguish these from poems simply written in couplets, we held to the widely accepted premise that, when traditional rhyme, repetition and metre are omitted, a ghazal can still be identified by what Kashmiri poet Aga Shahid Ali calls "a formal unity," and Thompson, "a matter of tone." However, given the number of beautiful ghazals we received, we were disappointed to find so few written in the traditional form. We hope that as the tradition becomes better known, perhaps partly through this book, more poets will try it.

We were surprised to find ourselves also having to draw lines around what constitutes a formal stanza. When we began our research, we dutifully saved what soon became an avalanche of poems written in stanza form. Certainly stanza is one of the signifiers of form, but we quickly decided it is probably the most widely (and casually?) retained formal aspect in the free verse tradition. If a poem had regular stanza breaks, but no additional pattern (such as metre, rhyme or repetition), we decided not to classify it as formal. So in the end, many poems we loved, that teased and tantalized like Anne Wilkinson's "Still Life," had to go. It was free verse, a poem deeply motivated by the formal elements of poetry, but free verse nonetheless.

When it came down to final choices for the book, once pattern, form and quality were established, the final test was oral. Often we read the poems to each other out loud and it was the ear, in the end, that decided whether we would include one poem over another.

This raised its own dilemma.

"Every revolution..."

There was one large category of poems with which we wrestled for some time. We were finding powerful poems, often strongly repetitive and chant-like, but we had no name for them and no apparent pattern or form other than this strong oral quality. Several times we dropped them, then scooped them back as being too memorable to let go. Finally we ran across the term "Incantation" in Lewis Turco's *The Book of Forms*, and we had a category where these poems could be placed together. Coming from widely different sources including Anglo-Saxon, Black and Aboriginal traditions, they reflect interestingly upon each other and upon the oral tradition.

However, anthologists seeking to print authentic poetry from oral traditions face specific difficulties. Historical Aboriginal songs, for instance, were collected primarily, if not entirely, by Europeans who, with all good intentions, understood the work in their own cultural context, and therefore missed subtleties. In addition, they often took extensive liberties by adding (European) rhyme and metre. As Daniel David Moses and Terry Goldie point out, historic work like the Inuit song in this anthology should be considered "samples of a recording process which comments on both cultures involved."[3] Further, the written renditions of this work cannot replicate its original oral presentation — the gestures, for instance, that go with the story behind the words.

Similarly, poets seeking to adapt these traditions to the printed page face particular challenges. Marlene Nourbese Philip, in the introduction to a collection of her poems, says her experience with writing from an oral tradition includes working on how "…to find some deeper patterning … of my language, the Caribbean demotic." She goes on to explain: "To keep the deep structure, the movement, the kinetic energy, the tone and pitch, the slides and glissandos of the demotic within a tradition that is primarily page-bound — that is the challenge."[4]

Expectations and surprises

The selection and editing process has been an intensely exciting one for us. For example, contrary to our expectations, we found that nineteenth century Canadian poets addressed far more than the stereotypical pastoral. We were delighted at the number of poems about politics, work and women's lives from that era. Also, when we began to place poems in sections, we discovered many that refused to be boxed into one form or another. Michael Redhill's "Haiku Monument for Washington, D.C." for example, is also a visual poem, Molly Peacock's ghazal "Of Night" is also a sonnet, and Phyllis Gotlieb's syllabic poem, "Death's Head" might as easily be considered incantation. There were many others, but one cross-over particularly puzzled us.

---

3   Moses, Daniel David and Terry Goldie, eds. *An Anthology of Canadian Native Literature in English*. Toronto: Oxford University Press, 1992, p. 368.

4   Philip, Marlene Nourbese. *She Tries Her Tongue, Her Silence Softly Breaks*. Charlottetown: Ragweed Press, 1989, p.23.

We kept finding poems — like Robyn Sarah's "Fugue" and Annie Charlotte Dalton's "The Praying-Mantis" — that sounded to the ear like form, with irregular but clearly repeating lines and phrases. But they couldn't quite be squeezed into any of the categories we had. Back and forth they went, from roundelay (for a repeating line), to stanza, to nonce (a form created by the poet for only one poem). It was Sandy who found it: "They're fugues!" she announced one day. Following the musical cue of Sarah's title, and in the finest (and oldest) tradition of poetry as music, we've gathered these poems together as a potentially emerging form, and grouped them with another long-standing fugal form in a separate chapter called "Fugue and Madrigal."

Overall, in making our selections, we have attempted to include nuggets many readers will recognize — such as Robert Service's "The Cremation of Sam McGee" — as well as less familiar poems, like Eric Duncan's "Drought." In addition, we've sought a balance between old and new, combining, wherever possible, nineteenth and early twentieth century examples with more contemporary work. We faced some limitations in this because the nineteenth century poems we found were primarily limited to couplets and tercets, stanzas, sonnets and ballads. Contemporary poets are expanding their reach to embrace a wider and more international selection of forms, such as the glosa, sestina, haiku and ghazal.

Many readers will be surprised to find we have included poets who are considered experimental, yet who clearly follow a given form. So, for example, bp Nichol and Christian Bök nestle up against the rhyme and metre of traditionalists like Archibald Lampman and Marjorie Pickthall. Everything old becomes new, they say. We find it exciting to see form in such new shapes.

Structure

We have organized this book in a way that, we hope, will illuminate poetic forms for both novice and experienced readers. Each chapter opens with a brief introduction to the form's origin and how it works, citing examples from the poems that follow to show how poets apply the tradition and the exciting ways they experiment with it. By necessity in such a short space, we've had to use many technical terms, so at the end we've included a chapter,

"Coming to terms," that explains the terminology of some of the key concepts used in this book and in prosody in general — line, metre, repetition and rhyme.

There is also an index and, for further reading, a list of reference books, many of which we relied upon heavily.

Two of these books warrant particular mention. We are not the first Canadians to record the formal tradition. Our forefather in this endeavour is Robin Skelton, whose posthumously published *opus magnum* is *The Shapes of our Singing: A Comprehensive Guide to Verse Forms and Metres from Around the World*. For years Robin taught poetry — and an awareness of form and metre — to students at the University of Victoria in British Columbia. His book is a compilation of established international forms, many of them little known in North America. Each form is illustrated by one of his poems. Another critical Canadian resource for us was Stephen Adams' *poetic designs: an introduction to meters, verse forms, and figures of speech*, which delves more deeply into, and beautifully explains, many elements of poetic craft.

We have no illusions that the book you now hold represents all the formal poetry or poets writing in Canada. For space reasons we've had to cut many of the fine poems we had in hand, and we're certain there are many more we're unaware of. And, as with any anthology, the twenty chapters here reflect our preferences, the forms we find most intriguing.

One aim of this anthology is to tap a well of interest in form — obviously a very deep one. Our hope is that this book will give readers and students insights into the way forms work, as well as offer ideas and inspiration to writers. In a field in which few things are entirely agreed upon, we also hope to generate discussion and further exploration of the fascinating world of poetic forms. But mostly we see this as a collection of Canadian poetry that will particularly please the ear as well as the heart. We hope it will bring back for all of us a (perhaps half-forgotten) pleasure in rhyme, repetition and rhythm.

BALLAD

Folk ballads are narrative poems that originated as songs sung by wandering minstrels in Europe during the fourteenth century or earlier. As part of an oral culture, these poems tended to change as they were passed along, so often there would be several versions circulating at any given time. Regardless of the version, however, all used simple, direct language to tell stories drawn from events such as a heroic act, a lost love, or the supernatural — and these features carried over to the written form.

While plot is generally more important than character in a ballad, poets often insert some dialogue to give a sense of the personalities involved and make the action more immediate. Robert Service, for instance, sprinkles "The Cremation of Sam McGee" with the occasional remark from McGee: "It's the cursed cold, and it's got right hold till I'm chilled clean through to the bone."

Repetition usually plays an important role in ballads. In "1838," Dennis Lee uses the refrain "Mackenzie comes again" at the end of each stanza to mark the transition from one aspect of the story to the next. In E.J. Pratt's "The Lee Shore," each reappearance of "come home" and "keep away" adds to the poem's emotional power. Whole stanzas can be repeated in various ways. In Bliss Carman's "Buie Annajohn," four of the seven lines in most stanzas are the same. The new lines develop the story and keep it moving forward, while the repeated lines build intensity.

Another common feature of ballads is the question and answer format used by Norah Holland in "The Grey Rider": "Why ride so fast through the wind and rain, / Grey Rider of the Shee? / Lest a soul should call for me in vain / Tonight, O Vanathee."

The traditional ballad stanza is a quatrain (four lines) rhyming *abcb* with four strong accents in the unrhymed (*ac*) lines and three in the rhymed (*b*) lines as in the following from Lee's poem:

"MacKenzie <u>had</u> a <u>print</u>ing <u>press</u>.
It's <u>soaking in</u> the <u>Bay</u>.
And <u>who</u> will <u>spike</u> the <u>Bish</u>op <u>till</u>
Mac<u>Kenzie comes again</u>?"

But poets freely improvise on this tradition. Two variations, an *abab* rhyme scheme and quatrains with four strong accents in every line, have become so common they are now considered standard.

Variations abound. Robert Service combines ballad stanza lines to create a longer line of seven strong accents with a couplet rhyme scheme plus an internal rhyme in every line ("It's the cursed *cold*, and it's got right *hold* …"). And John G. Fisher varies the form by ending "Back on the Job" with an extra two lines, which nicely complements the "extra roll" that ruined the bottle's neck.

THE TRADITIONAL FORM:

STANZAS:	An unlimited number of quatrains
METRE:	Alternating tetrameter and trimeter lines; or all tetrameter lines
RHYME:	*abcb* or *abab*
REPETITION:	Usually used extensively, often in the form of a regularly repeated phrase, line or stanza. (See "Coming to terms.")

Wilson H. Thomson
(b. 1800s)

THE CONTRACT MUCKER

When the dividend's set, I can say without doubt,
There is one man to thank when the cheques are sent out;
He's away down below where he can't see the sky
And he rarely complains, he's a hard working guy.
                    Is the mucker.

His shovel just burns when he's working below
It's a joy just to watch how he plays that banjo,
When the car's full of muck, with four wheels off the track
He just smiles and he says: "Oh alas and alack!"
                    Does the mucker.

When he's cleaned off the track, and he's got to the plate,
He will think the worst's over, but there, sure as fate,
He will find them all buckled, and bent, like a bow,
And instead of being flat, they are all in a row,
                    Does the mucker.

Then the sampler comes in, and he lays down his sheet.
And he says, "you must stop cos' I'm short fourteen feet"
But who is it says to sampler "do tell"
And will answer right smartly "you go plumb to hell".
                    It's the mucker.

They can say that a mucker is easily led,
That he's strong in the back, and he's weak in the head,
But that is a yarn that I cannot receive,
Because of one fact which you'll have to believe.
                    I'm a mucker.

When the sight of the bonus sheet knocks you all dead,
The sheet seems to set all the mines seeing red,
Then who is it, has the most sarcastic touch,
By informing the captain he's got far too much,
                    It's the mucker.

So upon his last shift when he's mucked his last round,
And he's up in the sky, where no shift boss is found,
When St. Peter has scanned the good book for his name,
And he says, "what are you" he can proudly proclaim,
                    "I'm a mucker."

———————

John G. Fisher
(b. 1800s)

BACK ON THE JOB

I sit once more at the glory hole,
     As I sat in days of yore,
And the charcoal flies in my face and eyes
     And oh! but my hands are sore.
There are blisters on my fingers
     And blisters on my thumbs,
And there are blisters every darned old place
     A blister ever comes.
My arms just feel like chunks of wood,
     I scarce can move them more,
But I sit and sing and roll my ring
     To the hum of the factory's roar.

The bottle is a sixteen ounce,
    It seems like sixteen pound,
As I drag it square upon the chair
    And roll it round and round.
I jab my tools in water
    I jab them in charcoal,
I jab them at the bottle's neck,
    But there! I've missed the hole;
And the bottle neck is a total wreck
    Because of an extra roll.

———————

Bliss Carman
(1861–1929)

BUIE ANNAJOHN

Buie Annajohn was the king's black mare,
Buie, Buie, Buie Annajohn!
Satin was her coat and silk was her hair.
Buie Annajohn,
The young king's own.
March with the white moon, march with the sun,
March with the merry men, Buie Annajohn!

Buie Annajohn, when the dew lay hoar,
(Buie, Buie, Buie Annajohn!)
Down through the meadowlands went to war —
Buie Annajohn,
The young king's own.
March by the river road, march by the dune,
March with the merry men, Buie Annajohn!

Buie Annajohn had the heart of flame,
Buie, Buie, Buie Annajohn!
First of the hosts to the hostings came
Buie Annajohn,
The young king's own.
March till we march the red sun down,
March with the merry men, Buie Annajohn!

Back from the battle at the close of day,
(Buie, Buie, Buie Annajohn!)
Came with the war cheers, came with a neigh,
Buie Annajohn,
The young king's own.
Oh, heavy was the sword that we laid on;
But half of the heave was Buie Annajohn,
Buie, Buie, Buie Annajohn!

Robert Service
(1874–1958)

THE CREMATION OF SAM MCGEE

There are strange things done in the midnight sun
By the men who moil for gold;
The Arctic trails have their secret tales
That would make your blood run cold;
The Northern Lights have seen queer sights,
But the queerest they ever did see
Was that night on the marge of Lake Lebarge
I cremated Sam McGee.

Now Sam McGee was from Tennessee, where the cotton blooms and blows,
Why he left his home in the South to roam 'round the Pole, God only knows.
He was always cold, but the land of gold seemed to hold him like a spell;
Though he'd often say in his homely way that "he'd sooner live in hell."

On a Christmas Day we were mushing our way over the Dawson trail.
Talk of your cold! through the parka's fold it stabbed like a driven nail.
If our eyes we'd close, then the lashes froze till sometimes we couldn't see;
It wasn't much fun, but the only one to whimper was Sam McGee.

And that very night, as we lay packed tight in our robes beneath the snow,
And the dogs were fed, and the stars o'erhead were dancing heel and toe,
He turned to me, and "Cap," says he, "I'll cash in this trip, I guess;
And if I do, I'm asking that you won't refuse my last request."

Well, he seemed so low that I couldn't say no; then he says with a sort of moan:
"It's the cursed cold, and it's got right hold till I'm chilled clean through to the bone.
Yet 'tain't being dead — it's my awful dread of the icy grave that pains;
So I want you to swear that, foul or fair, you'll cremate my last remains."

A pal's last need is a thing to heed, so I swore I would not fail;
And we started on at the streak of dawn; but God! he looked ghastly pale.
He crouched on the sleigh, and he raved all day of his home in Tennessee;
And before nightfall a corpse was all that was left of Sam McGee.

There wasn't a breath in that land of death, and I hurried, horror-driven,
With a corpse half hid that I couldn't get rid, because of a promise given;
It was lashed to the sleigh, and it seemed to say: "You may tax your brawn and brains,
But you promised true, and it's up to you to cremate those last remains."

Now a promise made is a debt unpaid, and the trail has its own stern code.
In the days to come, though my lips were dumb, in my heart how I cursed that load.
In the long, long night, by the lone firelight, while the huskies, round in a ring,
Howled out their woes to the homeless snows — Oh God! how I loathed the thing.

And every day that quiet clay seemed to heavy and heavier grow;
And on I went, though the dogs were spent and the grub was getting low;
The trail was bad, and I felt half mad, but I swore I would not give in;
And I'd often sing to the hateful thing, and it hearkened with a grin.

Till I came to the marge of Lake Lebarge, and a derelict there lay;
It was jammed in the ice, but I saw in a trice it was called the "Alice May."
And I looked at it, and I thought a bit, and I looked at my frozen chum;
Then "Here," said I, with a sudden cry, "is my cre-ma-tor-eum."

Some planks I tore from the cabin floor, and I lit the boiler fire;
Some coal I found that was lying around, and I heaped the fuel higher;
The flames just soared, and the furnace roared — such a blaze you seldom see;
And I burrowed a hole in the glowing coal, and I stuffed in Sam McGee.

Then I made a hike, for I didn't like to hear him sizzle so;
And the heavens scowled, and the huskies howled, and the wind began to blow.
It was icy cold, but the hot sweat rolled down my cheeks, and I don't know why;
And the greasy smoke in an inky cloak went streaking down the sky.

I do not know how long in the snow I wrestled with grisly fear;
But the stars came out and they danced about ere again I ventured near;
I was sick with dread, but I bravely said: "I'll just take a peep inside.
I guess he's cooked, and it's time I looked"; … then the door I opened wide.

And there sat Sam, looking cool and calm, in the heart of the furnace roar;
And he wore a smile you could see a mile, and he said: "Please close that door.
It's fine in here, but I greatly fear you'll let in the cold and storm —
Since I left Plumtree, down in Tennessee, it's the first time I've been warm."

> *There are strange things done in the midnight sun*
> *   By the men who moil for gold;*
> *The Arctic trails have their secret tales*
> *   That would make your blood run cold;*
> *The Northern Lights have seen queer sights,*
> *   But the queerest they ever did see*
> *Was that night on the marge of Lake Lebarge*
> *   I cremated Sam McGee.*

———————————

Norah M. Holland
(1876–1925)

THE GREY RIDER

Why ride so fast through the wind and rain,
        Grey Rider of the Shee?
Lest a soul should call for me in vain
        To-night, O Vanathee.

Now, whose is the soul shall seek thine aid,
        Grey Rider of the Shee?
The soul of one that is sore afraid
        To-night, O Vanathee.

O fears he the flurry of wind and rain,
        Grey Rider of the Shee?
More deep is the dread that sears his brain
        To-night, O Vanathee.

Does he fear the tumult of clanging blows,
        Grey Rider of the Shee?
Nay, darker still is the fear he knows
        To-night, O Vanathee.

Does he fear the loss of wife or child,
        Grey Rider of the Shee?
Nay, a terror holds him that's still more wild
        To-night, O Vanathee.

O what should make him so sore afraid,
        Grey Rider of the Shee?
He fears a wraith that himself has made
        To-night, O Vanathee.

Then how shall you cleanse from fear his mind,
        Grey Rider of the Shee?
I will touch his eyes, and they shall be blind
        To-night, O Vanathee.

Yet still may he know the voice of fear,
        Grey Rider of the Shee?
I will touch his ears that he shall not hear
        To-night, O Vanathee.

Yet that wraith may linger around his bed,
        Grey Rider of the Shee?
No terror shall touch the quiet dead
        To-night, O Vanathee.

E.J. Pratt
(1883–1964)

THE LEE-SHORE

Her heart cried out, — "Come home, come home,"
When the storm beat in at the door,
When the window showed a spatter of foam,
And her ear rang with the roar
Of the reef; and she called again, "Come home,"
To the ship in reach of the shore.

"But not to-night," flashed the signal light
From the Cape that guarded the bay,
"No, not to-night," rang the foam where the white
Hard edge of the breakers lay;
"Keep away from the crash of the storm at its height,
Keep away from the land, keep away."

"Come home," her heart cried out again,
"For the edge of the reef is white."
But she pressed her face to the window-pane,
And read the flash of the signal light;
Then her voice called out when her heart was slain,
"Keep away, my love, to-night."

Dennis Lee
(b. 1939)

1838

The Compact sat in parliament
To legalize their fun.
And now they're hanging Sammy Lount
And Captain Anderson.
And if they catch Mackenzie
They will string him in the rain.
And England will erase us if
Mackenzie comes again.

The Bishop has a paper
That says he owns our land.
The Bishop has a Bible too
That says our souls are damned.
Mackenzie had a printing press.
It's soaking in the Bay.
And who will spike the Bishop till
Mackenzie comes again?

The British want the country
For the Empire and the view.
The Yankees want the country for
A yankee barbecue.
The Compact want the country
For their merrie green domain.
They'll all play finder's-keepers till
Mackenzie comes again.

Mackenzie was a crazy man.
He wore his wig askew.
He donned three bulky overcoats
In case the bullets flew.
Mackenzie talked of fighting
While the fight went down the drain.
But who will speak for Canada?
Mackenzie, come again!

———

Ryan Knighton

(b. 1972)

THE BALLAD OF ECHOLOCATION

Lighthouse the slick line
a spearing the far sky
for catching the capsize
a shipment of import.

The ocean a body
of mine is the tiding
to slacken the water
the mouth is a coastline.

The old beach a comber
of fingers the trawling
the chancing a gathering
of flesh cut the mooring.

Lighthouse the slick line
a spearing the far sky
for catching the capsize
a shipment of import.

The labour an anchor
of water the secret
the definite nation
a buoy on the last day.

The gutting a chumslop
of fish the alarming
a notion the skullcap
of ocean the longing.

Lighthouse the slick line
a spearing the far sky
for catching the capsize
a shipment of import.

The deep is the hollow
of shell pitched the captain
the whistling a not there
mayday in the once ear.

BLUES

The blues — a uniquely African-American form of folk song — evolved in the nineteenth century from the work songs of southern black slaves who used traditional African rhythms to express feelings of grief and loss over the conditions of their lives. The music evolved using flattened third, fifth and seventh notes (known as "blue" notes).

The *New Grove Dictionary of Music and Musicians* points out that "since the sixteenth century 'the blue devils' has meant a condition of melancholy or depression." The subject matter of blues music was often loss — death or love lost — and the love was usually the physical kind; in this, it was clearly secular and distinguished from spirituals. But no matter what the subject, the ability to express a blues feeling is key to the form.

As with any oral tradition adapted to the page, blues poetry varies widely, but generally, following the twelve-bar sequence of the music, it is written in any number of three-line stanzas with four strong accents in each line. The second line repeats or slightly varies the first, giving a singer time to find a third, rhyming line that responds to the emotion of the first two, often with a wry twist of humour. This tension before the elaboration in the final line is reminiscent of the turn in an Italian sonnet, or the final couplet of the English one.

The blues rhyme scheme is usually *aaa* or (less often) *aab*, and as befits the oral tradition, images tend to be vividly graphic.

In "Conjured," R. Nathaniel Dett uses a less common blues style of four lines with two strong accents per line — "I'm <u>con</u>jured! I'm <u>con</u>jured!" — for an eight bar blues. George Elliott Clarke, who brought this poem to our attention, describes it as possessing a syncopated, fast-moving "ragtime" feel. Clarke's own "King Bee Blues" picks up on the theme of raunchy love ("But don't be surprised / If I sting your flower today"), and when his six line stanzas are compressed to three lines, they follow standard blues rhyme and metre. Bruce Meyer's "The Diet" is a blues sonnet because it uses the sonnet tradition of fourteen lines with five strong accents in most lines, as well as the blues traditions of an *aaa* rhyme scheme and near-repetition of first and second lines with a response in the third. Perhaps most importantly, the poem evokes the "blues" feeling.

One of the origins of blues was a collective "call-and-response" (and later, individual "hollers"), that helped set a pace for heavy rural labour. Wayde Compton's "Jump Rope Rhyme for the 49er Daughters" applies the traditional call-and-response technique to the California gold rush days of 1849. At the other end of the spectrum, his "Alley Blues" and Christine Wiesenthal's "blues," push the form to its modern limits. Although neither has regular stanza, repetition or rhyme schemes, both keep to an oral rhythm and the lost love theme of blues. "blues" is also a prose poem that plays with "bluing" — a process traditionally used to prevent whites from going yellow in the wash.

THE TRADITIONAL FORM:

STANZAS:	An unlimited number of tercets (sometimes quatrains)
METRE:	Tercets usually have 4 strong accents per line, and quatrains, 2 strong accents per line; 5 strong accents per line are also common
RHYME:	*aaa* or *aab*
REPETITION:	Line 1 is often repeated exactly or with a slight variation in line 2; this anticipates and delays the response of line 3, which often uses humour to expand the meaning of the stanza

R. Nathaniel Dett
(1882-1943)

CONJURED

Couldn't sleep last night!
   Just toss and pitch!
I'm conjured! I'm conjured!
   By that little witch!

My heart's all afired!
   My brain's got the itch!
I tell you I'm conjured
   By that little witch!

I'm "patchy" in feelings;
   It seems that a stitch
Has sewed me up inside out.
   Then there's a hitch

Whenever I try to think;
   Side track and switch
My thoughts do; and finally
   Dump me in the ditch.

And when I talk, my voice
   Seems all out of pitch;
When I think about her,
   My pulses, they twitch.

I'm in love or I'm crazy,
   I can't tell quite which;
But I know I've been conjured
   By that little witch!

F. R. Scott

(1899–1985)

METRIC BLUES

Mile, gallon and pound
root me in solid ground,
but metre, litre and gram!
Lhude sing goddamm!

    Kill that smile
    you measured mile.
    The metric talon
    's got you, gallon.
    Frown, pound,
    you're quite unsound.

Metre, litre and gram!
Lhude sing goddamm!

    Oh heck
    gone is the peck.
    Never again
    a chain.
    No more search
    for the tricky perch,
    and the innocent yard
    is barred.

Metre, litre and gram!
Lhude sing goddamm!

Yell and flinch
ell and inch.
Shudder and scram
Rood and drachm.
Poor pole
you've lost your role
and your daily bounce
ounce.
Pints and quarts?
You're torts!

Metre, litre and gram!
Lhude sing goddamm!

Furlongs, fathoms and rods
dead as the old gods.
Not so much as a stone
for an anglophone
alone.

Lhude, lhude sing
goddamm!

Frederick Ward

(b.1937)

WHO

Who gonna bargain for my soul
Who gonna bargain last

Her mouth stretched
withered and flush:
the crimson what come'd
round a bruise

though the voice
be a high sparrow-chirping:
the sudden flutter-ups-of-a-
startled thing

When she gripped a lone note
a breeze neath silk
be of report
and carried the thought of a

modest young girl
stooped to press her apron
gainst her dress
ironing it from the heat of her thighs

then standing erect
— surrounded by ancient
yet courageous tremblings.
shouts:

Who gonna bargain for my soul
Who gonna bargain last

Maureen Hynes
(b. 1948)

SELF-SUFFICIENT BLUES

Workin girl, I wake up every day
with the wanna-stay-in-beds
Workin girl, I wake up every day
fix my house instead.

Got the self-sufficient blues, got them down fine.
Got the self-sufficient blues, just me, myself and mine.
It's the fix my own plumbing, tie my own shoes,
make my own decisions, paint my own blues.

Got my education, got my medication,
got my job down pat.
Got my education, got my medication,
got a therapist and a cat.

Got the half a head of lettuce, the salad greens go bad.
Got the full fridge, empty table, one wineglass sads.
Got the self-sufficient blues, the flying solo crime
Goin through the motions and I'm getting by just fine.

But what's missing is some kissing,
a pair of boots inside my door.
What's missing is some kissing
a little laughin' and l'amour.

Got the self-sufficient blues, got the me, myself and mine.
Got the self sufficient blues, oh I carry on just fine.

Bruce Meyer
(b. 1957)

THE DIET
for Barry Callahan

Living a little seems like dying slow.
Living a lot is better than dying slow.
      Let's have more of everything before we have to go.

Loving a little is preferred to dying slow.
Loving a lot and you forget you're dying slow.
      Babe, let's do something before we have to go.
      Let's have more of everything before we have to go.

Needing a little feels like dying slow.
Needing a lot is the same as dying slow.
      Let's have more of everything before we have to go.
      O Babe, let's do it all before we have to go.

Dying a little is better than living slow.
Dying a lot is just like living slow.
      Don't say I didn't warn you. Now it's time to go.

———————

George Elliott Clarke
(b. 1960)

KING BEE BLUES

I'm an ol' king bee, honey,
Buzzin' from flower to flower.
I'm an ol' king bee, sweets,
Hummin' from flower to flower.
Women got good pollen;
I gets some every hour.

There's Lily in the valley
And sweet honeysuckle Rose too;
There's Lily in the valley
And sweet honeysuckle Rose too.
And there's pretty, black-eyed Susan,
Perfect as the night is blue.

You don't have to trust
A single Black word I say.
You don't have to trust
A single Black word I say.
But don't be surprised
If I sting your flower today.

Christine Wiesenthal
(b. 1963)

BLUES

"If these tests fail, depend only on an expert. You will save money, time and worry by calling a reliable service organization for a man who knows your appliance thoroughly."
— Home Laundry Guide

what is this weakness that washes over me as I sort through *the blues* always make me think of the sight of his denim clad hips sauntering along in slim cut *jeans* jeans old jeans good jeans his jeans my jeans a combination *I like to fantasiz*e about pants a couple pair crumpled in a heap tangled legs pockets peeled inside out in haste *slip in* four socks and some lightly scented soap *like ABC* things get out of hand though and the agitator starts churning my gut to slush sucks me into his spin and puts me through the wringer till I find myself all washed up and hung up and strung out on a long thin line or two *flap flap flapping* on about a load of *nothing at all* can console me now *as Dinah Washington sings* I'm seeing red and feeling blue/holding my breath waiting for you *sucker* just can't wait to see him again *can you* maybe get in the last lick *this time* breezing along out the blue give him a smack on the cheek a smart wet one too

Wayde Compton
(b. 1972)

JUMP ROPE RHYME OF THE 49ER DAUGHTERS

caller got a treasure map and a silver pick.
all how you gonna know where to dig?

caller map got a great big X on it.
all how you gonna know where to dig?

caller got 10 paces marked in black.
all how gonna know where to dig?

caller gonna count em off ...
all 1, 2, 3, 4, 5 — gonna count em off.

caller gonna count em off...
all 6, 7, 8, 9 ,10 — gonna count em off.

caller gonna count em off ...
all 1, 2, 3, 4, 5 — gonna count em off.

caller gonna start again ...
all 6, 7, 8, 9, 10 — gonna count em off.

caller got a treasure map with a silver spade.
all how you gonna know where to dig?

caller just like a pirate with a wooden leg.
all how you gonna know where to dig?

caller girl in the middle gotta spell her name ...
all how you gonna know where to dig?

caller	jumpin on one foot, okay?
all	jumpin on just one foot.

girl	A-l-e-x-a-n-d-r-i-a.
all	how you gonna know where to dig?

Wayde Compton
(b. 1972)

ALLEY BLUES

no congregation. pasts to shake.
to lose.

no going back. just space to take
up. fools

      running

the place. renting us
ramshackle truths.

        alley blues.

at the terminal

call
for alcohol. in our own

dark
town, night
trips. falls
on us

     down

in what
always. is

      dark town.

COUPLET

The simple couplet — two consecutive rhyming lines — has been one of the most widely used English poetic forms since it was introduced by Geoffrey Chaucer in *The Legend of Good Women* and *The Canterbury Tales*. Although, like the tercet, it's not usually considered a stanza form in its own right, the couplet can serve as one when used, for example, in the epigram and ghazal.

The three most common couplet forms are closed, open and heroic, all of which rhyme *aa*. In a closed couplet both sense and syntax are complete within the two lines, and this is often marked by punctuation that shows either a stop or pause. For example, in Robert Finch's "Egg-and-Dart," the first couplet is clearly closed: "This never-ended searching for the eyes / Wherein the unasked question's answer lies." An open couplet carries its sense forward to the next line or lines, as in the transition from the first to second couplet of Christopher Wiseman's "April Elegy" ("... Eighty-eight this time and so // Alive, thank God"). Most poets agree that the heroic couplet is closed and written in iambic pentameter, as in Jay Macpherson's "The Third Eye."

The couplet's power comes from its compression and intensity. Given this power, it's no surprise that it is widely incorporated into other forms, such as the English sonnet and the ghazal. But no matter where it's used, the form demands a creative use of rhyme and a good ear to keep it from falling into a dull sing-song rhythm.

Consistent with its long lineage, the couplet embraces many variations, one of which is the short couplet, written in lines with four strong accents, as illustrated by Sir Charles G. D. Roberts' "The Skater" ("My glad feet shod with the glittering steel"). Wiseman's poem is a one-time nonce form of open couplets, with a loose iambic metre and an *ab* rhyme scheme that comes from almost always using the same two end-words ("way" and "go"). Daniel David Moses abandons metre, but keeps a traditional *aa* rhyme scheme and skillfully uses open couplets to provide momentum in "The Fall."

THE TRADITIONAL FORM:

STANZAS:	Two lines each, no set number (not usually considered a stanza form)
METRE:	Heroic couplets are in iambic pentameter; short couplets are in iambic tetrameter; otherwise the pattern is optional
RHYME:	*aa*
REPETITION:	None required
DISTINGUISHING FEATURE:	Closed couplets are complete in sense and syntax; open couplets use enjambment

Sir Charles G. D. Roberts
(1860–1944)

THE SKATER

My glad feet shod with the glittering steel
I was the god of the wingèd heel.

The hills in the far white sky were lost;
The world lay still in the wide white frost;

And the woods hung hushed in their long white dream
By the ghostly, glimmering, ice-blue stream.

Here was a pathway, smooth like glass,
Where I and the wandering wind might pass

To the far-off palaces, drifted deep,
Where Winter's retinue rests in sleep.

I followed the lure, I fled like a bird,
Till the startled hollows awoke and heard

A spinning whisper, a sibilant twang,
As the stroke of the steel on the tense ice rang;

And the wandering wind was left behind
As faster, faster I followed my mind;

Till the blood sang high in my eager brain,
And the joy of my flight was almost pain.

Then I stayed the rush of my eager speed
And silently went as a drifting seed, —

Slowly, furtively, till my eyes
Grew big with the awe of a dim surmise,

And the hair of my neck began to creep
At hearing the wilderness talk in sleep.

Shapes in the fir-gloom drifted near.
In the deep of my heart I heard my fear.

And I turned and fled, like a soul pursued,
From the white, inviolate solitude.

Barker Fairley
(1887–1986)

BACH FUGUE

This is the first of the themes, the lecturer said,
Please be at pains to fix it in the head,

Or else you'll miss the beauty. Now the next,
So different and so subtly interflexed,

And now the third (I forget if there were ten;
To tell the truth, I had forgotten then).

And remember to listen across as well as along,
It's a Bach fugue you'll hear and not a song.

The voice stopped short. And then there was a pause
With screwing of faces remembering rules and laws.

I remembered nothing. The fingers touched the keys,
And I travelled across and along with a swimmer's ease.

Robert Finch
(1900–1995)

EGG-AND-DART

This never-ended searching for the eyes
Wherein the unasked question's answer lies;
This beating, beating, beating of the heart
Because a contour seems to fit the part;
The long, drear moment of the look that spoils
The little bud of hope; the word that soils
The immaculate pact, so newly born;
The noisy silence of the old self-scorn;
These, and the sudden leaving in the lurch;
Then the droll recommencement of the search.

Jay Macpherson
(b. 1931)

THE THIRD EYE

Of three eyes, I would still give two for one.
The third eye clouds: its light is nearly gone.
The two saw green, saw sky, saw people pass:
The third eye saw through order like a glass
To concentrate, refine and rarify
And make a Cosmos of miscellany.
Sight, world and all to save alive that one
Fading so fast! Ah love, its light is done.

———————

Christopher Wiseman
(b. 1936)

APRIL ELEGY (SAM SELVON D.1994)

I call my mother on her birthday, the way
I always do. Eighty-eight this time and so

Alive, thank God. I can hear her smile. She may,
She says, for this is morning there, go

To the shops later. We talk about the way
She feels, the way England is, her chance to go

And visit her sister. Family talk. The way
We do. I miss her. I miss others. Go

Back when I can. You went a different way,
Sam, old smiler — this time you were asked to go

Back to Trinidad, famous there now, way
Past time. And you were pleased, you said, to go.

I sometimes met you in the shops here, the way
People meet, and we talked of how it was to go,

After the war, to London, alone, and the way
You survived, the jobs, how you made money go

Further in your long exile. The way
You told it, you'd enjoy yourself and go

Collect people and places there, learn the way
You had to write them, make them speak, go

On giving time to lives, pointing a way.
Why were we both in exile? Why did we go

Walkabout from our roots? We discussed the way
Of the world, journeying, the push to go.

You stop on my mother's birthday — nice the way
You did that, like a writer — more shops to go

To, more good talk untalked, and she, way
Across the ocean, this spring day, will go,

My mother, healthy, eighty-eight, the way
She does, to her shops. But you never said you'd go.

Never told me that, like this, you'd go.

———————————

Timothy Brownlow
(b. 1941)

JAMES CLARENCE MANGAN
IN TRINITY COLLEGE LIBRARY

His weary eyes watch lanterns in the square
Squeak in wind, papers blown about the air,

Great trees dishevelled by the sudden squall,
Which woke him from his dream behind the wall

Of books, bound books that he knows little of
Except the few which fire his frenzied love

And keep him from his cataloguer's task,
(And like the busts, his face a pallid mask.)

The snug alcove where he preferred to work
Was near the sightless gaze of Swift and Burke,

But his rage was of other kind than theirs.
Stiffened with alcohol, he sought the stairs

And stumbled out of eighteenth-century grace,
Across the cobbles, dreaming of a race

As yet unborn, or dead so long he saw
The merest ghosts emerge from history's maw,

And racked by drugs and dreams, like Baudelaire,
He walked the city of his heart's despair,

Across the river, up to his dark den,
And lit his candle, coughed, took up his pen

And wrote some verse that morning would not spare
(The pale sky showed the dawn already there)

Until, defeated, he snuffed out the flame
and with it seemed to blow away his fame.

Tomorrow, Berkeley, Swift, glue, ink and dust,
And madness winking at him from a bust.

———————

Eric Ormsby

(b. 1941)

JAHAM SINGS OF THE FEAR OF THE MOON

The moon is thin with fear,
the delicate moon is thinner than despair.

The fear of the moon is the fear of the hare
curved in its burrow when the fox is near.

The fear of the moon is the fear of the fog
(The fog is afraid of the fox and the dog

and the moon is afraid of all three.)
The moon is a thorn in midnight's tree.

The moon is thin as the edge of a cry,
as fine as the side of a word.

The thin moon hides in the dark of my eye.
Night-hidden I heard

its thinness crackle like the stalks of fall
before the hail comes and the first stars fall.

Night-hidden I heard its thin feet run
away from the golden horror of the sun.

———

Daniel David Moses
(b. 1952)

THE FALL

Apples glow
deliciousness across the long furrow

puddles where last night's
rain rivulets or sits

and clears, accepting the old
afternoon light. The mud halfway there holds

on so to the black rubber
boots that the picture

book falls open
faced and even in

a sock the child's foot is
naked to the splash. His cries

stream out like wordless
questions and the crow who passes

quickly through the open
seems to mimick them.

EPIGRAM

Epigrams are brief, witty poems defined more by their tone than their formal structure. Dating back to ancient Greece, epigrams are usually rhymed and typically have two parts. The first part states the theme and the second features a turn that makes the point with a quick, impressive flourish, often using satire or humour to do so. The following epigram by Coleridge provides both a definition and a good example of the form: "What is an epigram? A dwarfish whole; / Its body brevity, and wit its soul."

These small gems seem capable of anything. They will as readily praise, commemorate or compliment (as in Richard Outram's "Tourist Stricken At the Uffizi"), as ridicule, censor or insult (as in the anonymous "Bugs").

When composed as inscriptions for monuments or gravestones (regardless of whether they are, in fact, engraved in stone) epigrams like the one in this chapter by Robert Finch are known as epitaphs.

Epigrams are usually no more than eight lines and can stand alone as one or more stanzas, or be part of a longer poem. Although usually rhymed and metered, they can be equally effective in free verse, as shown by Margaret Atwood's sardonic "[you fit into me]" and Dionne Brand's indignant "Winter Epigram: 21."

THE TRADITIONAL FORM:

STANZAS:	Usually a maximum of 8 lines; sometimes broken into stanzas
METRE:	Often iambic pentameter, but the metric pattern (if any) is up to the poet
RHYME:	Often *aa* or *abab*, but the rhyme scheme is up to the poet
REPETITION:	None required
DISTINGUISHING FEATURE:	An observation with a clever twist; easy to remember

Robert Hayman
(1575–1629)

from QUODLIBETS

The foure Elements in Newfound-land. To the Worshipfull Captaine John Mason,
who did wisely and worthily governe there divers yeeres.

The Aire, in *Newfound-Land* is wholesome, good;
The Fire, as sweet as any made of wood;
The Waters, very rich, both salt and fresh;
The Earth more rich, you know it is not lesse.
Where all are good, *Fire, Water, Earth, and Aire,*
What man made of these foure would not live there?

To a worthy Friend, who often objects the coldnesse of the Winter in Newfound-Land,
and may serve for all those that have the like conceit.

You say that you would live in Newfound-land,
Did not this one thing your conceit withstand;
You feare the *Winters* cold, sharp, piercing ayre.
They love it best, that have once wintered there.
Winter is there, short, wholesome, constant, cleare,
Not thicke, unwholesome, snuffling, as 'tis here.

...

To all those worthy Women, who have any desire to live in Newfound-Land, specially
to the modest & discreet Gentlewoman Mistris Mason, *wife to Captaine* Mason,
who lived there diverse yeeres.

Sweet Creatures, did you truely understand
The pleasant life you'd live in *Newfound-land*,
You would with *teares* desire to be brought thither:
I wish you, when you goe, faire wind, faire weather:
For if you with the passage can dispence
When you are there, I know you'll ne'r come thence.

---

anon
(early pioneer)

BUGS

Each year when the vile bugs come round
To feast on my potatoes,
I let them taste the Paris green,
I give it to them gratis.

They eat it, sicken, and they die;
Death stops them in their mission:
'Tis just what every bug deserves
That eats without permission.

F. R. Scott
(1899–1985)

BRÉBEUF AND HIS BRETHREN

When Lalemant and de Brébeuf, brave souls,
Were dying by the slow and dreadful coals
Their brother Jesuits in France and Spain
Were burning heretics with equal pain.
For both the human torture made a feast:
Then is priest savage, or Red Indian priest?

Robert Finch
(1900–1995)

from FOUR EPIGRAMS

Epitaph

Here lies a man who was so bright
He beat the very flight of light,
There was no ditch he could not clear
Except the one he lies in here.

A. J. M. Smith
(1902–1980)

NEWS OF THE PHOENIX

They say the Phoenix is dying, some say dead.
Dead without issue is what one message said,
But that has been suppressed, officially denied.

I think myself the man who sent it lied.
In any case, I'm told, he has been shot,
As a precautionary measure, whether he did or not.

Dorothy Livesay
(1909–1996)

GOING TO SLEEP

I shall lie like this when I am dead —
But with one more secret in my head.

Raymond Souster

(b. 1921)

VERY SHORT POEM

"… But only God can make a tree."

(He'll never try it in Sudbury.)

Richard Outram

(1930–2005)

TOURIST STRICKEN AT THE UFFIZI

Dear God, for the rest of my life:
And how shall I tell her, my wife,
That the pallor of a Botticelli Venus
Has come, irrevocably, between us?

Alden Nowlan
(1933–1983)

AUNT JANE

Aunt Jane, of whom I dreamed the nights it thundered,
was dead at ninety, buried at a hundred.
We kept her corpse a decade, hid upstairs,
where it ate porridge, slept and said its prayers.

And every night before I went to bed
they took me in to worship with the dead.
Christ Lord, if I should die before I wake,
I pray thee Lord my body take.

———————

Margaret Atwood
(b. 1939)

[YOU FIT INTO ME]

you fit into me
like a hook into an eye

a fish hook
an open eye

———————

Dionne Brand
(b. 1953)

from WINTER EPIGRAMS

21.

so I'm the only thing you care about?
well what about the incursions into Angola,
what about the cia in Jamaica,
what about El Salvador,
what about the multi-national paramilitaries
in South Africa,
and what do you mean by "thing" anyway?

FUGUE AND MADRIGAL

Derived from the Latin *fuga*, meaning flight, the fugue may well be an emerging poetic form. In music, a fugue is a polyphonic (or multi-voiced) composition rich in counterpoint (the interweaving of melodies). Originating in choral music, it usually involves three or four voices. A fugue begins with one voice introducing a brief melody called the subject. While the first voice goes on to present a counter subject, a second answers with the original melody, and so on until all are singing. The voices then take off in various directions, as if chasing one another across related keys, approaching and straying from the original subject, reinventing it as they go. The devices used to modify the subject include changing its rhythm and/or presenting it a few tones higher or lower than its previous appearance.

This is adapted to poetry through inventive uses of repetition, which can range from elaborate to relatively simple — but always unpredictable — constructions. In particular, themes are introduced in phrases or lines that are then reiterated, in full or in part, throughout the poem, shifting context, pace and meaning.

Robyn Sarah, in an interview with Canadian poet Stephen Brockwell,[5] says she "intuitively created" the form for her "Fugue," as a one-time approach to a particular subject. "Only after it was finished did I notice the pattern in which the repeating lines change their position from stanza to stanza ... the *pattern* of repetition was indeliberate, it was dictated by ear." In private correspondence[6] she said she only later became aware of Paul Celan's "Todesfugue."[7] American poet Dana Gioia, on the other hand, specifically searched for a way to adapt the musical fugue to formal poetry. In *Ecstatic Occasions, Expedient Forms*, he says it took him years to write his poem "Lives

---

5   The interview is online at www.poetics.ca #3.

6   Robyn Sarah, in correspondence with the editors, February 2004.

7   "Todesfugue" can be found in *Selected Poems and Prose of Paul Celan*. Translated by John Felstiner. New York: Norton, 2001, p. 30.

of the Great Composers," noting: "The one example I knew of, Paul Celan's magnificent 'Todesfuge,' was too unique and lofty a model to provide any specific help, though its existence proved that the form could be approximated in verse."

To our knowledge, none of the poets included in this chapter deliberately wrote their poems to be fugues as such. What they have in common is how they draw from a wide range of repetition devices to mix and match, arrange and rearrange images and ideas with an insistence that gives the poems their power as well as their unique form. Gwendolyn MacEwen in "The Children Are Laughing," for example, repeats phrases at the ends of consecutive lines or at the end of one line and the beginning of the next ("they believe they are princes" and "the children are laughing"), lending a sense of urgency to the poem.

The different approaches these poets take to rhyme, stanza and metre suggest a wide range of possibilities for a fugue. Milton Acorn, for instance, uses an irregular rhyme scheme while Annie Charlotte Dalton writes in rhymed couplets. Acorn and MacEwen use a loose metre, while Sarah and Herménégilde Chiasson write in free verse.

In music, the madrigal is a fugal form, usually sung without accompaniment. It was most popular from the fifteenth to seventeenth centuries and focused on secular rather than sacred themes. Aaron Copland, in *What to Listen For in Music*, says it is a "typical vocal fugal [form] of the era before the advent of Bach and his contemporaries."[8]

In poetry, the madrigal dates back hundreds of years and takes several forms. Those included in this chapter, by Marilyn Bowering and Robin Skelton, follow the form that Lewis Truco, in *The New Book of Forms*, says was invented by Geoffrey Chaucer in the fourteenth century.

THE TRADITIONAL FORM

Fugue
STANZAS: An unlimited number of stanzas
METRE: No set metre or syllable count required

---

8   Copland, Aaron. *What to Listen for in Music*. New York: Penguin (A Mentor Book), 1999, p. 142.

| RHYME: | No rhyme scheme required |
| REPETITION: | Two or more themes are introduced, each contained in a line or phrase that usually appears early in the poem; all are then repeated unpredictably, in part or in full and in any order, throughout the poem; usually various repetition devices (see "Coming to terms") are also employed |

Madrigal (Chaucerian)

STANZAS:	Three stanzas; the first is a tercet; the second, a quatrain; the third, a sestet
METRE:	Iambic pentameter
RHYME:	Stanzas have different rhyme schemes: the tercet is AB^1B^2; the quatrain is $abAB^1$; the sestet is $abbAB^1B^2$ (capital letters stand for refrains, numbered capitals — e.g., B^1B^2 — indicate rhymed, but otherwise different, refrain lines)
REPETITION:	The tercet provides the poem's three refrains; the first refrain is line 1, repeated as lines 6 and 11; the second is line 2, repeated as lines 7 and 12; the third is line 3, repeated as line 13

Annie Charlotte Dalton
(1865–1938)

THE PRAYING-MANTIS

In the dark dungeons of the mind;
Strange creatures walk and breed their kind;
    The Mantis mounts the stair,
    With movements free as air.

The Praying-Mantis mounts the stair,
Her tiny arms upheld in prayer.
    In chasuble and stole,
    She stands to read my soul.

I know not what dark thing is there,
Nor why my soul must feel despair,
    Nor why she turns away
    And bids the Mantis slay.

In the deep dungeons of the mind,
Strange creatures walk and breed their kind;
    With arms upheld in prayer
    The Mantis mounts the stair.

———————

Milton Acorn
(1923–1986)

THE BALLAD OF THE PINK-BROWN FENCE

Against the pink-brown fence with the sprucelet
My little sister stands to be photographed;
Fire tinges from her head and the dandelions —
Tear down the pink-brown fence to make a raft

Tear down the pink-brown fence to make a raft
Where my little sister stands to be photographed
Fish poke up their noses and make rings
And memories of dandelions dance from the ripples . . .

The camera is too slow to catch the gold
of dandelions remembered around my little sister;
Stand up the old raft for a painting board
And guess the why of it — you can't recall kissing her . . .

Cut up the rotten painting for a bonfire;
The flames rush up a rattle, faint boom, and whisper;
Sparks fly gold in the night and then white;
Dandelions, and the hair of my little sister

———————

Gwendolyn MacEwen
(1941–1987)

THE CHILDREN ARE LAUGHING

It is Monday and the children are laughing
The children are laughing; they believe they are princes
They wear no shoes; they believe they are princes
And their filthy kingdom heaves up behind them

The filthy city heaves up behind them
They are older than I am, their feet are shoeless
They have lived a thousand years; the children are laughing
The children are laughing and their death is upon them

I have cried in the city (the children are laughing)
I have worn many colors (the children are laughing)
They are older than I am, their death is upon them
I will wear no shoes when the princes are dying

———————

Herménégilde Chiasson
(b. 1946)

AND THE SEASON ADVANCES
(translated by Jo-Anne Elder & Fred Cogswell)

And the season advances
The radios are louder
The trees are taller than they were
The sky is whiter
And the season advances
The day gets shorter
The trees are whiter
The sky is more beautiful
The street is wider than it was
And you cry out to me
And I run towards you untiringly
It is ridiculous
I know
But the season advances
The day gets shorter
It is ridiculous
I know

— Moncton, 1968

Robyn Sarah
(b. 1949)

FUGUE

Women are on their way
to the new country. The men watch
from high office windows
while the women go.
They do not get very far
in a day. You can still see them
from high office windows.

Women are on their way
to the new country. They are taking
it all with them: rugs,
pianos, children. Or they are leaving
it all behind them: cats,
plants, children.
They do not get very far in a day.

Some women travel alone
to the new country. Some
with a child, or children.
Some go in pairs or groups
or in pairs with a child
or children. Some in a group with
cats, plants, children.

They do not get very far in a day.
They must stop to bake bread on the road
to the new country, and to share
bread with other women. Children
outgrow their clothes and shed them
for smaller children. The women too
shed clothes, put on each other's

cats, plants, children, and at full moon
no one remembers the way to the new country
where there will be room for everyone and
it will be summer and children will
shed their clothes and the loaves will
rise without yeast and women will have come
so far that no one can see them, even from

high office windows.

———————

Robin Skelton
(1925–1997)

NIGHT PIECE

I have been dreaming half the night
of holding you beside the sea
and watching waves crash into light.

I do not know how I can write
of that heart-pounding mystery;
I have been dreaming half the night
of holding you beside the sea

and wondering if those breakers might
be telling of our times to be
when tide and moon are at their height;
I have been dreaming half the night
of holding you beside the sea
and watching waves crash into light.

———

Marilyn Bowering
(b. 1949)

MADRIGAL, A LULLABY FOR XAN

She sleeps, her dreams as clear as diamond edge
that cuts the icy sky in black and white,
the stars are palest candles to her light.

The dark spills over sill and window ledge,
a river foaming bleakly through the night.
She sleeps, her dreams as clear as diamond edge
that cuts the icy sky in black and white.

The wren that sings its heart-song through the sedge,
and braves the hunter hawk in its full flight,
dreams of its mate and nest soon in its sight:
she sleeps, her dreams as clear as diamond edge
that cuts the icy sky in black and white,
the stars are palest candles to her light.

GHAZAL

The ghazal is a form of lyric poetry that originated in Arabia, probably around the seventh century. Originally it consisted of at least three and no more than eleven couplets, although today it's generally accepted as from five to twelve couplets written in a given rhyme and metre, so that every line is about the same length. Its spirit is one of great intensity and compression, somewhat like the Japanese haiku, although — unlike the haiku — the ghazal relies heavily on metaphor. Traditional ghazal couplets were never enjambed; in fact, they were so independent of each other their order could be changed without damaging the poem. Kashmiri poet Agha Shahid Ali (1949-2003), who perhaps did most to introduce the traditional form into English, explains in *Ravishing DisUnities* that the unity of the ghazal flows from both its pattern of rhyme and refrain, and from its tone and intensity, so that, in his words, "There is a contrapuntal air."

Some of the ghazal's most famous practitioners were Ghalib in India, and the Persian, Hafiz (a fourteenth century contemporary of Chaucer's). Traditionally, poets used the ghazal to write about love — both mystical and carnal. Nadeem Parmar, who writes contemporary ghazals in Urdu, says the praise of women and wine in the original form was always done in a very "delicate and civilized manner," much like the troubadours who were writing courtly love poems to women in Europe at around the same time.[9] The ghazal was introduced into Europe in 1812 with a German translation of Hafiz, and remains a vibrant form (often put to music) in many languages, including Arabic, Urdu, Farsi and Hindi.

Yvonne Blomer's "Landscapes and home" is an example of a traditional (although unmetered) ghazal. None of the seven couplets are enjambed and the first sets the tone and pattern for the rest of the poem. The word "home"

---

9   Ron Padget, in *The Teachers & Writers Handbook of Poetic Forms*, comments that, "The troubadours were travelling French poet-musicians, some of them noblemen or crusader-knights, who flourished from the end of the eleventh century through the thirteenth century. The female counterparts of the troubadors were called trobairitiz" (p. 175).

that ends both lines of this couplet is the refrain that also completes the second line of every couplet thereafter. This refrain (which may also be a phrase) is preceded by a mono-rhyme ("takes," "makes," "claim" and so on). The rhyme acts as a cue to listeners who, when they hear it, traditionally join the poet and call out, with much shared pleasure, the concluding refrain in each couplet. (In this way the aural power of the ghazal is similar to that of the rhyme in closed couplets, which also provides notice to listeners that something is coming to an end.) The last two lines of the traditional ghazal are a signature couplet in which the poet has the option of signing his or her name (or a pseudonym), as Blomer does when she opens the final line with "Yvonne."

Kuldip Gill and Sina Queyras take some liberties with the tradition. In "Ghazal V," Gill uses the refrain "turned loose" in all but the opening line and usually precedes it with the identical rhyme "is." Queyras, in "Tonight the Sky Is My Begging Bowl," takes an innovative approach to the refrain by using various forms of the word "sleep" ("sleepless," "sleepy" etc.). She precedes it with an assonance rhyme ("brick," "picket," "winter" etc.). Molly Peacock makes a different leap, this time into the tradition, when she writes "Of Night" in a loose iambic metre, omits spaces between the couplets, repeats the refrain ("of night" or "at night") in every line, and uses a preceding mono-rhyme ("paws," "jaws," "laws," etc.). She calls this fourteen-line variation a "ghazal sonnet."

North American poets who first adopted the ghazal form in the twentieth century, including John Thompson in Canada and Adrienne Rich in the U.S., largely ignored the form's tradition. But without rhyme or refrain, and with liberal enjambment between couplets, what differentiates a ghazal from any free verse poem written in couplets? In the introduction to his book, *Stilt Jack*, Thompson answers by saying, "the link between couplets … is a matter of tone, nuance … its order is clandestine … It is the poem of contrasts, dreams, astonishing leaps."[10] Thompson wrote what might be called "free verse ghazals" which omit the traditional repetition, rhyme, metre and (to a large extent) similar line length.

---

10   Thompson, John. *John Thompson: Collected Poems and Translations*. "Introduction" to *Stilt Jack*. Fredericton: Goose Lane, 1995, pp. 105-6.

Patrick Lane, one of many who follow Thompson's example, originally wrote the poem, "I walk to the river in deep snow ..." as a ghazal, but later refined his sense of this and other poems in his book, *A Linen Crow, A Caftan Magpie*. In a postscript to that collection, he said "The form is not the ghazal, though I deluded myself for a time thinking it was. It is rather a composite of the haiku and ghazal, a resemblance and nothing more, perhaps more oriental than occidental."[11] But his poem keeps the unity of the ghazal form by using no enjambment between couplets and by maintaining a consistency of tone — what poet Lorna Crozier calls a "sense of urgency and darkness."[12]

THE TRADITIONAL FORM:

STANZAS:	Usually 5 to 12 (or more) closed couplets (*shers*). The first couplet (*matla*) sets the tone and pattern for the rest of the poem
METRE:	Each line is approximately the same length and can be metered
RHYME:	*aa ba ca* and so on, plus an internal mono-rhyme (*qafia*) immediately before the refrain in each couplet
REPETITION:	The refrain, either a word or phrase (*radif*), ends both lines of the opening couplet, and is repeated as the end of the second line of each succeeding couplet
DISTINGUISHING FEATURE:	The poet uses his or her name or a pseudonym in the final signature couplet (*mukta*)

11   Lane, Patrick. *A Linen Crow, A Caftan Magpie*. Saskatoon: Thistledown Press, 1984.
12   Crozier, Lorna. "Dreaming the Ghazal Into Being," in *Bones in their Wings*. Regina: Hagios Press, 2003, p.55.

Phyllis Webb

(b. 1927)

from SUNDAY WATER

Ten white blooms on the sundeck.
The bees have almost all left. It's September.

The women writers, their heads bent under the light,
work late at their kitchen tables.

Winter breathes in the wings of the last hummingbird.
I have lost my passion. I am Ms. Prufrock.

So. So. So. Ah — to have a name like *Wah*
when the deep purple falls.

And you have sent me a card
with a white peacock spreading its tail.

———————

Kuldip Gill

(b. 1934)

GHAZAL V

My white mare on the Punjabi plains, the stamp of her hooves
marks the borders of my land as she is turned loose.

It's the morning of her wedding. How tightly they braid her hair.
Now her doria are swinging; in hours they will be his, turned loose.

A swing hangs in the pipal tree. Baisaki: flowers yellow and gulabi.
From the roof top khoti the cucurooing doves have been turned loose.

The white stallion savours a mouth without bit and bridle.
Off with his saddle! A slap on the flanks and he is turned loose.

The doli swings as guests watch the bride leave her natal village.
Bristling with coir, the coconut in the groom's lap is turned loose.

Awake Vasanti! His imposters under gowns of virtue. On love's
wings, the phoenix by his flaming heart is turned loose.

John Thompson
(1938–1976)

from STILT JACK

IX

Yeats. Yeats. Yeats. Yeats. Yeats. Yeats. Yeats.
Why wouldn't the man shut up?

The word works me like a spike harrow:
by number nine maybe I get the point.

It's all in books, save the best part; God knows
where that is: I found it once, wasn't looking.

I've written all the poems already,
why should I write this one:

I'll read Keats and eye the weather too,
smoke cigarettes, watch Captain Kangaroo.

Big stones, men's hands, the shovel
pitched properly. The wall of walls rises.

If I weren't gone already, I'd lie down right now:
have you ever heard children's voices?

Sometimes I think the stars scrape at my door, wanting in:
I'm watching the hockey game.

Likely there's an answer: I'm waiting,
watching the stones.

———————————

Patrick Lane
(b. 1939)

from A LINEN CROW, A CAFTAN MAGPIE

I walk to the river in deep snow. The ice is thick.
In the heart of the city. Drunk and singing.

At least be happy.
Excellence in the small. Tears frozen on your face.

Lie with me here. We will make cold angels.
Dig inside words but don't hide your head there.

Why are you most happy when happiness fails?
Under the ice, fat fish, beaver, rat.

Molly Peacock
(b. 1947)

OF NIGHT

A city mouse darts from the paws of night.
A body drops from the jaws of night.
A woman denies the laws of night,
Awake and trapped in the was of night.
A young man turns in the gauze of night,
Unravelling the cause of night:
That days extend their claws at night
To re-enact old wars at night,
Though dreams can heal old sores at night
And Spring begins its thaw at night,
While worry bones are gnawed at night.
He sips her through a straw at night.
Verbs whisper in the clause of night.
A finger to her lips,
                        the pause of night.

Lorna Crozier
(b. 1948)

EXCELLENCE IN THE SMALL.
TEARS FROZEN ON YOUR FACE.

Winter: *eat the little, talk a lot* —
that's magpie's definition.

Tears freeze on the cheeks and
never fall. This is cold, not sadness.

Somewhere warmer, Vallejo said
we must learn

a different way of weeping. For now,
the old way will have to do.

———————

Sina Queyras
(b. 1963)

TONIGHT THE SKY IS MY BEGGING BOWL

While I savour woodstove-scented sleep,
you move in a forest of brick and glass: sleepless.

Your eyes droop, dreaming the half-point of grades
and coffee at the end of the picket line. Sleepy.

I dress in fleece, stalk blackberries for birds,
canes flattened from a winter storm as we slept.

I embrace everything, even the slither of midnight,
but without you, time is too wide, I cannot sleep.

Clatter of dragon paw — the old year retreats, tail between
her legs. This thumping new one will not sleep.

We are simply where we are. Me, alone
in silk and fleece, you on a subway deprived of sleep.

Tonight the sky is my begging bowl: wing tip,
wood thrush I open palms, heart, enclave of sleep.

Yvonne Blomer
(b. 1970)

LANDSCAPES AND HOME / GHAZAL 22

In the dark, there, our eyes. Landscapes and home.
We traveled by boat, ship, finally a plane takes us home.

This webbing feeds memories, the recesses
Where we can name everything, makes a home.

Here is always different: Harare, Bindura.
In Canada, even, we move, try to claim a home.

The rising sun, or no sun, instead a blanket of rain
the body comes back to itself, wakes at home.

Piles of leaves or sand dunes — green battles brown.
If I blow a kiss, pressed lips snake home.

Home is hot or wet, a bird's nest:
dead-dry stalks, green leaves, a make-believe home.

Who am I? My body, this traveling thing.
Yvonne, each thread of memory aches of home.

GLOSA

Originating in the late fourteenth to early fifteenth century Spanish courts, the glosa is a delightful way for poets to exchange or build upon one another's ideas in a structured poetic form. And, particularly since the publication of P.K. Page's *Hologram, A Book of Glosas*, numerous Canadian poets have taken up such conversations.

A glosa normally has four ten-line stanzas preceded by four lines quoted from another poet (this quatrain also acts as a kind of epigraph to the poem). Each stanza ends with a line taken sequentially from the borrowed quatrain. While there is no required metre, lines 6, 9 and 10 of each stanza are end-rhymed.

The glosa picks up on the concept of glossing — that is, elaborating or commenting on a text (alternate names for the form are *gloss* or *glose*). In her introduction to *Hologram*, Page notes, too, that she used the glosa "as a way of paying homage to those poets whose work I fell in love with in my formative years." [13]

One of the delights of a glosa rests in the process of writing toward the borrowed lines. The poet, in expanding on these lines, is working with something intrinsic to the other author's words, something both share. This goes beyond technique; to quote Page, it's like "a curious marriage — two sensibilities intermingling."

Poets often vary the form slightly — for instance, by making some or all stanzas shorter than the standard ten lines, as in Brenda Leifso's "What do you want?" (Interestingly, a glosa written entirely in quatrains has a similar repetition pattern to the rondeau redoubled described in the Rondeau Family chapter.) Another variation is when poets use the opening lines to form part, rather than all, of a stanza's final line, as in Aaron Pope's and Jodi Shaw's "Revelation."

---

13 Page, P. K. *Hologram, A Book of Glosas*. Toronto: Brick Books, 1994, pp. 9-10 (the quotation in the next paragraph is from p. 9).

At the other end of the spectrum, the glosa can be made even more elaborate. Glenn Kletke, in "O Grandfather Dust," does this by doubling the form. Working from an eight-line quotation, each subsequent stanza begins with a line taken consecutively from the first four lines and ends with one from the last four.

THE TRADITIONAL FORM:

STANZAS: An opening quatrain from another poet, plus 4 10-line
                stanzas
METRE: No set metre or syllable count required
RHYME: Lines 6, 9 and 10 are end-rhymed
REPETITION: Each line of the opening quatrain reappears once, in order,
                to close each of the other four stanzas (i.e., line 1 of the
                quatrain is also line 10 of the first stanza, and so on)

P. K. Page
(b. 1916)

PLANET EARTH

> *It has to be spread out, the skin of this planet,*
> *has to be ironed, the sea in its whiteness;*
> *and the hands keep on moving,*
> *smoothing the holy surfaces.*
>
> *"In Praise of Ironing," Pablo Neruda*

It has to be loved the way a laundress loves her linens,
the way she moves her hands caressing the fine muslins
knowing their warp and woof,
like a lover coaxing, or a mother praising.
It has to be loved as if it were embroidered
with flowers and birds and two joined hearts upon it.
It has to be stretched and stroked.
It has to be celebrated.
O this great beloved world and all the creatures in it.
It has to be spread out, the skin of this planet.

The trees must be washed, and the grasses and mosses.
They have to be polished as if made of green brass.
The rivers and little streams with their hidden cresses
and pale-coloured pebbles
and their fool's gold
must be washed and starched or shined into brightness,
the sheets of lake water
smoothed with the hand
and the foam of the oceans pressed into neatness.
It has to be ironed, the sea in its whiteness

and pleated and goffered, the flower-blue sea
the protean, wine-dark, grey, green, sea
with its metres of satin and bolts of brocade.
And sky — such an O! overhead — night and day
must be burnished and rubbed
by hands that are loving
so the blue blazons forth
and the stars keep on shining
within and above
and the hands keep on moving.

It has to be made bright, the skin of this planet
till it shines in the sun like gold leaf.
Archangels then will attend to its metals
and polish the rods of its rain.
Seraphim will stop singing hosannas
to shower it with blessings and blisses and praises
and, newly in love,
we must draw it and paint it
our pencils and brushes and loving caresses
smoothing the holy surfaces.

———————

Patrick Lane
(b. 1939)

THE GARDEN TEMPLE

Tell me every detail of your day —
When do you wake and sleep, what eat and drink?
How spend the interval from dawn to dusk?
What do you work at, read, what do you think?

"The Answer," P. K. Page

No one comes to this garden. The dawn
moves through the bamboo beside the bridge.
It's quiet here and I'm alone. The small nun
who led me has drifted behind the screen
and I'm quiet as I watch a slender mallard
drift on the pond into first light. She is two birds,
one above and one below. Night and day,
and night was long again. You are far away.
Tell me every detail of your day.

Now more than ever I miss your hands,
your small feet, the slight swell of flesh in the dark,
the breath you hold before crying out.
I'm trying to remember that sound but I don't know
what time it is in the place you are.
The small nun appears and disappears
behind the paper screen. She moves slowly now
and I can't hear her as I once did. This garden is how she thinks.
When do you wake and sleep, what eat and drink?

Solitude is presence. It is the absence
I live in now. How long have we lived apart?
A week, a month, a year? It all feels the same.
Time doesn't move but for the day and the night
moving like a curtain behind the maples. I imagine your hand
on a yellow curtain by a window in the room
where you sleep. The mallard has slipped into shadow
where eelgrass meets sand below the arbutus.
How spend the interval from dawn to dusk?

I don't know. There are nights I go for long walks
in the narrow, twisting streets and stare
at the bare lights in windows as they flare,
then I come back to my room in the dark
and I sit in the dark for long hours.
How far away. Here there is water and leaves
and I think of your hands and feet, a yellow curtain,
a room of light, or is it dark there now?
What do you work at, read, what do you think?

——————

Glenn Kletke

(b. 1942)

O GRANDFATHER DUST

And did you come there in summer, tobogganing in the slow sheets
Of earliest love; come there to work your secret name
On the frozen time of a wall; and did you come there riding
The tall and handsome horse whose name's Catastrophe.

(O grandfather dust!) thick and mousetracked, leads to rooms
Without character: boxes of boxed darkness: birdshit —
(But only the swallow nests here — the daubs of mud over doorways
Are the most live things in the house.)

"Letter to an Imaginary Friend," Thomas McGrath

And did you come there in summer, tobogganing in the slow sheets
of a child's week at the farm, the welcome of morning
as you stepped into a world you knew nothing of? Sharp sun!
Call of barnyard animals! Shape of a grandfather slouching
at the edge of things: rake, fork, pail in his grasp or nothing
at all — hands cupped to hold above prairie wind, prairie blooms
the frail struggling life inside a rolled cigarette (Player's blue tin)
or whirled through air — terrifying — a long poplar's stick to flick
his two work horses to bright fields from barn's dark tombs.
(O grandfather dust!) thick and mousetracked, leads to rooms

Of earliest love; come there to work your secret name
notched once on a poplar tree, hardly knowing what
you were called, bringing into the world only the hunger
to learn the calling of others: how she would open
the torn screen door, grandmother with a heap of potato
peels, chickens running madly towards her call, exquisite
pandemonium as they picked and fled with flopping treasures
to safer ground, how later in the morning you would carry to her
(O grandmother ashes!) prairie smoke, its spidery flower a misfit
Without character: boxes of boxed darkness: birdshit —

On the frozen time of a wall; and did you come there riding
    on the slow and gentle horse of a child returning, hooves
    hardly heard through fields of blue flax on a summer afternoon?
    Silent gallop back to a gilded farm house filled with whatever
    wonders your universe once held: wood stove, piled logs, pail
    of well water (cold, so cold), tin dipper, sky dipper, Milky Way
    Farmers Weekly (German), wall of windmills, windows of geraniums
    the brilliant red cockscomb of a rooster sun going down.
    Now you look everywhere for anything to fill the dark days
(But only the swallow nests here — the daubs of mud over doorways

The tall and handsome horse whose name's Catastrophe.
    See its saddle notched with farm's felled four-footed souls:
    May and Nel (horses too), Dollie and Peg (cows), Nipper
    Yogi, beagle-shadowed Rex (first and best mongrel of the pack)
    and Sox, grey cat stolen from the city to prowl the prairie
    white elegant boots and too courtly to catch a mouse.
    Now through cracked windows fly the six-footed bees, peeling
    yellow wall a flower that spiders them, your knowledge that whole
    generations of dead workers heaped on the ground like a shot ruffled grouse
Are the most live things in the house.)

Betsy Struthers

(b. 1951)

LAST DAYS

She felt the flower of his pain beneath her hand
which cupped for it and was soft and yearned as if
all her blood had withdrawn to the stamping wrist
and her hand was wax, wanting the pain in it

"The Flower and the Rock," P. K. Page

She could have told him a million times and tried
how it felt for her to watch him as she did
puttering in the garden, his peak hat
tipped to one side, the red braces he wore
now he doesn't remember what a belt is for
slipping off his shoulders as he bends. A man
who knew the Latin names for herbs,
dreaming in the garden, fingers on his fly.
She slapped his arm to make him understand.
She felt the flower of his pain beneath her hand

though he barely flinched, her touch that familiar
to him and that light. She cried and when he asked her
what was wrong, his chapped lips trembling,
she said she had been stung. A white lie, another
in the string of all she had to tell to keep him whole
and hers. Each day he wakened by her one more gift
though there were nights she thought of single beds
he thrashed so, cried out in his sleep, disturbing her.
And yet, to hug his wasted frame against her hip
which cupped for it and was soft and yearned as if

erotic love were possible, was enough; too soon
she'd be sleeping on her own, the double bed half
empty. She zipped him up and nagged him,
knowing even as she did he had not forgotten,
he really did not know why he must do that
or this. He pouted, he pleaded: "Miss,"
he called her, as if she were a teacher or a nurse,
someone to look after him, look out for him. All
her worry had crumpled her long fingers into fists,
all her blood had withdrawn to the stamping wrist

and the blue vein convulsing in her throat. She
had to swallow screams, she couldn't let out
what it meant to her to have him and yet have not.
He stroked a parsley leaf and called it "soap,"
knelt, scratched at patio stones to plant a spoon.
"Potato," he looked at her and said. She had to sit,
her hand on her heart, her overflowing heart
that skipped, but still beat on. He sat beside her,
took her hand in his and put it to his lips. And bit,
and her hand was wax, wanting the pain in it.

———————————

Aaron Pope and Jodi A. Shaw
(b. 1975 & 1982)

REVELATION

> *Back to the quiet, knowing*
> *these terrible iron tongues*
> *no longer hammer*
> *against the walls of my house.*

> *"Coming Back," John Thompson*

Frogs and crickets
crinkle the night,
shoot scat. The cats purr
and torture birds
in the back acre bush.
I went driving today, rolled
the windows down, stopped
for fiddleheads in Fredericton,
got lost driving home   on the only known road
back to the quiet, knowing.

The house is harvested
among sounds, it shrugs.
I strip the walls,
pull the nails,
the lath, the plaster,
on the floor in piles of dust
to dust. I do not have the tools to fix this mess. I
do not know how to revive what I have
killed. I cannot build. All the dead among
nails and bullets and words — *these terrible iron tongues.*

I wrote nothing
serious today, just
five glosas and a *guzzle*
a day keeps the doctor away. I know
these are lies. Terry
tells stories and shouts at his camera.
He shouts what he's found. *The secret,*
he says, *is never believe*
a word I say. Truth is a mantra
I *no longer hammer.*

Thirty-three and all I have: a rifle,
five hunting knives, a matchbook,
muddy boots at the back door, a pile of
paper and ink stains — no firewood.
Why is it so dark? So goddamn cold.
Tired. Drunk. *In this place we might be happy:*
we might have been.
It is all in pieces, ruins, piles on the floor:
the things we could not hold
repelled *against the walls of my house.*

Brenda Leifso
(b. 1977)

WHAT DO YOU WANT?

want the apple on the bough in
the hand in the mouth seed
planted in the brain want
to think "apple"

from *Naked Poems, Phyllis Webb*

want back my thick tongued
child's rage, white eye light,
whole body burn, feet
drumbeat against that wall against
silence, want fruit in my belly
in my throat want the room
to speak, with my hands to sing,
to touch that eclectic finger
want to be loved before forgiven
want the apple on the bough in

the beginning. again.
and. again. want a poem
where hunger moves beyond
sound beyond naming
breast thigh stomach. want grief
burnished by plum blossoms
thrown skywards,
rain in my skin sea
in the hand in the mouth seed

caught in silk,
stored in the greenhouse until spring
or until i am wise enough
or clever enough to tell a story new
until that time, the greenhouse will stay warm
and this time, i will watch sod
born from my grandmother's hands
turning, opening, i will watch her
spread light like sundogs
planted in the brain, want

that warmth in my mouth:
mulch of fern soft fig
star fruit peeled plum
pomegranate
fingers all juice and flesh
for the bough reaching,
throat unfastened, able at last
to think "apple."

David Reibetanz
(b. 1982)

NORGBERTO HERNANDEZ –
PHOTOGRAPHED FALLING SEPTEMBER ELEVENTH
A Glosa for P. K. Page

> *Warmed by that same summer sun.*
> *But the dead of the near dead*
> *are now all knucklebone*
> *Whoever is alone will stay alone.*
>
> "Autumn," P. K. Page

The picture wants to be upside down, head
first like the falling man. Air ripples
skin at that speed. Yet he was not calm water
as he jumped, nor crumbling grit blown out
by the blast. In his last choice
he spoke his mother tongue.
White shirt caressing him,
he rejected flame's touch.
Yet he too was one
warmed by that same September sun.

Puerto Rican pastry chef,
sweating, he rode
the subway, his cool patrons
in Mercedes passing him above. But
when the moment came, he went
as he was, dispossessed, shed
no corporate skin — flying
past them, his path chosen,
no end ahead
but the dead, or the near dead.

Near dead, plummeting
a free unfallen man,
the chute of his life opens.
He knows a grace of air,
spiralling against
lines of the metalled glass pantheon.
Godlike, he spins
in the mind. His hands —
unbound, become his own —
are now all kucklebone.

Freed in a lasting moment,
he falls, right leg over left,
pirouetting
towards death. What is it
he sees, eyes closed
ears open to the wind's undertone?
Beyond fear now, he rides
the light. Pouring himself into
the lens of our eye, he lives in unison:
we make his sun-drenched blue our own.
Whoever is at one will never stay alone.

HAIKU AND OTHER JAPANESE FORMS

In the west, some of the best known Japanese forms include haiku, renga, tanka, senryu and haibun. Probably the best known of these is the haiku (or hokku, meaning "starting verse"). In Japanese, haiku consist of three unrhymed lines of 5, 7 and 5 sounds (called *onji*). The form originated as the first part of a renga, a group composition in which one poet wrote a verse of 5, 7, 5 sounds and handed it to a second poet, who added a verse of 7, 7, which created and completed a tanka. This was then passed on to the next poet, who added a verse of 5, 7, 5 and so on, to create the renga. The haiku became a form in its own right in the hands of Basho (1644-1694).

The English syllable, however, is not an exact equivalent of the Japanese sound it aims to duplicate. William Higginson, in *The Haiku Handbook*, notes that in English, about twelve syllables — not seventeen — approximates the equivalent length of sound in the Japanese language; accordingly, although many modern haiku writers in English write haiku in three lines of 5, 7 and 5 syllables, others often use fewer, as in Marianne Bluger's haiku sequence, "Leafsmoke." Regardless of syllable count, at some point there is often a pause in both rhythm and grammar that divides the haiku into two parts (and the five-line tanka usually includes a break in syntax after the second or third line).

Traditional haiku aim to unite nature with human nature through objective rather than subjective or lyric description. They use a season word *(kigo)* indicating the time of year (such as "burnt fields" or "bare oaks" in Bluger's "Leafsmoke"), a seasonal theme *(kidai)*, sketch a singular event in the present tense, convey a sense of awe or transcendence and evoke, rather than overtly describe or name, emotion. The form relies on clear, concrete images rather than simile or metaphor and generally makes minimal use of articles. The goal is a sudden insight or meditation. As one of its great Japanese practitioners, Yosa Buson (1716-1783) described it, haiku "use the commonplace to escape the commonplace."[14] Traditionally, they were not given titles.

Originally, all Japanese poetry including haiku was written vertically. Michael Redhill echoes this tradition as well as the concept of visual poetry in "Haiku Monument for Washington, D.C." which repeats a single word (vertically) five, seven and five times.

Senryu follow the haiku form but focus on human nature and are more light-hearted, as in Rita Wong's initial senryu in "Leavetaking."

Haibun are brief, minimalist prose pieces, often journals or travel diaries, often humourous or light-hearted. They end with one or more haiku and give a renga-like effect when written in a series. There is no obvious connection between the prose and closing haiku; the connection is left to the reader to decode. Fred Wah varies the haibun by ending it with what might be considered the haiku equivalent of a prose poem.

The tanka, which dates back as far as the seventh century, was a dominant poetic form in Japan until about the fourteenth century, when the renga replaced it in popularity. By the nineteenth century, however, the form revived and now flourishes in Japan and many other countries. Traditionally its themes were primarily, though not restricted to, nature and love, and it tended to be written in long sequences. Much later, in Europe, the sonnet would follow in the tanka's footsteps to play a role in courtship.

The haiku sequence — several haiku on a common subject — was, like the tanka, being written long before Petrarch ever composed a sonnet sequence. Here, David McFadden combines senryu and tanka in one sequence, and Brian Bartlett — as his title suggests — "shuffles" the same words to create a sequence of very different haiku that echo the quality of anagrams.

THE TRADITIONAL FORM:

STANZA: Three lines (which also serve to open the tanka and renga, and close the haibun)

---

14   Jean Hyung Yul Chu, "Haiku," in *An Exaltation of Forms*, p.217.

METRE:
- Haiku and senryu lines have a syllable count of 5, 7, 5 or less in English; a pause in both rhythm and grammar divides them into two parts
- Tanka lines have a syllable count of 5, 7, 5, 7, 7 or less in English; usually there is a break in syntax after the second or third line
- The opening prose paragraph of the haibun is unmetered

RHYME: Not rhymed

REPETITION: None required

Winona Baker
(b. 1924)

from SPRING

in the pocket
of his woodshed coveralls
a nest of deer mice

Henry Beissel
(b. 1929)

TANKA

ice rain coats berries
keeping the bluejays away
till summer's necklace
snaps and casts glittering black
pearls before lazuli nights

Fred Wah

(b. 1939)

FATHER/MOTHER HAIBUN #5

You can't drive through a rainbow I said hills to myself in
the mountains glory of a late summer early fall thunder
storm the Brilliant Bluffs brilliant indeed the shine rain and
sunshine waves of science breaking lickety split school
systems memory for the next word after colour from the
other side no one could see it otherwise nature's path is
home to the bluebird triangular son/event/father w/ time-
space China rainbow over your youth vertical like on the
prairies that rainbow stood straight up into the sky on the
horizon you'd think in the winter sun ice crystals could
form unbelievable

**Radio on, up north an American hunter shoots a rare
white moose, geese in the sky, nibbling ribbons**

———————

David W. McFadden

(b. 1940)

SHOUTING YOUR NAME DOWN THE WELL

Beside my bedside —
Takuboku's "Poems to Eat"
Placed by dear old friends.

*

Late at night I sit
Watching the fish in the tank.
Their eyes never close.
They're like little wind-up toys.
Wonder if they know they're real.

*

Ian sees I am
Torturing myself again.
I tell him if I
Don't torture myself who will?
He says give nature a chance.

*

Everyone has a
Shitty time of it in life.
A fly in a web
Watching the spider approach —
How is it different from me?

*

Since I discovered
Takuboku my fingers
Are numb with counting.

———————

Marianne Bluger
(b. 1945)

LEAFSMOKE

fogbound
in a hotel room
reruns …

a scorched smell —
burnt fields in the rain
the boulders steam

in a dark window
Dad's pale face
watching our bonfire soar

darkness
moving in among the pines
a screen-door slams

mad shadows
— a moth at the porchlight —
I grip a cold key

bald from chemo
my friend Diana
a laughing Buddha

this rainy night
out wandering anywhere
the wet leaves point

between the waxen corpse
and massed mums
someone sobs

calling
the geese leave
sadness

after the burial
only rain & bare oaks
distancing in rearview

cloudy afternoon
a white chrysanthemum
just one

down a wet street
the funeral cortège
of someone important

bitter words
in the dark — sleet
hitting our windshield

through the slot
with the pizza flier
a cold gust

———————

Colin Morton
(b. 1948)

from HORTUS URBANUS / URBAN GARDEN

Twice now this morning I am wakened by full-throated geese
Veeing over my roof. How is a poet to dream through this?
      High in the wind-torn white pine a cardinal pipes his
claim to all he surveys. From chimneytop the crow replies
sharply. In cedar branches sparrows watch a blue jay splash in
the water.

        Fleet light, how do you
    taste? How have you left no tracks
        in reaching this place?

———————

Brian Bartlett
(b. 1953)

SHUFFLES
for Rosemary and Ricky Talbot

winter blooms, turns
and throws across snow
shadows, light, leaves, a child

                    winter leaves turn and
                    a child blooms, throws
                    snow light across shadows

across light blooms and leaves
winter throws turns,
snow shadows a child

                    snow light throws blooms
                    across winter: a shadow child
                    turns and leaves

                    *

hear the story leap
and the breath whisper
and roar through you

                    story the breath
                    and hear you roar
                    and leap through the whisper

breath through story:
you roar the whisper and
hear the leap and —

> you hear, whisper and leap
> and roar the breath
> through the story

George Elliott Clarke
(b. 1960)

HYMN FOR PORTIA WHITE

The white, bathing moon
      ogles itself in the sea,
            all black and handsome.

Michael Redhill
(b. 1966)

HAIKU MONUMENT FOR WASHINGTON, D.C.

RomeRomeRomeRome
RomeRomeRomeRomeRomeRome
RomeRomeRomeRome

Rita Wong
(b. 1968)

LEAVETAKING

empty coathangers
clash. echo in the closet.
he will not return.

I walk with the spring
lightness of bare feet after
a winter of boots

INCANTATION

The word incantation comes from the Latin root *cantare*, to sing. *The Canadian Oxford Dictionary* defines it as "a magical formula chanted or spoken." In poetry, incantations make up a broad category that includes chants, charms and spells. Their strong appeal is often based on oral performance.

Although many forms of poetry use repetition, incantation relies heavily on rhythmic insistence to create an intensely emotional, mesmerizing effect for magic or ritual purposes. It overtly appeals to the senses, especially the ear, and to the body's physical pleasure in repetition.

Common techniques include repetition of a final word or phrase, as in bp Nichol's playful "Turnips Are," and repetition of an initial word or phrase, as in the Inuit poet Aua's song, "To Lighten Heavy Loads," where the persistent, "I will ... I will ..." reinforces the walker's resolve.

Sir Charles G. D. Roberts' "Autochthon" and Jon Furberg's "Nightspell" both echo ancient runes — magical signs or sounds once used for charms. Roberts gives voice to ancient spirits of the land ("I am the spirit astir") and Furberg, calling upon the magical power of words, casts his "Nightspell" through the drum-like repetitive sounds and stresses of Anglo-Saxon prosody (described in the final chapter): "Wounding words, whetted on flesh."

Incantation can also be achieved in list poems (also known as catalogue poems) that cite a rhythmic accumulation of details, as in Brenda Brooks' chant, "Life, Having Become Still."

Greg Scofield chants in his original Cree ("ôh, êkwa kâ-kimiwahk, kâ-kimiwahk") and even for those of us who cannot speak Cree, the magic of pure sound adds emphasis to the power of the incantation.

THE TRADITIONAL FORM:

STANZAS: Any number of stanzas of any length
METRE: May or may not be metered
RHYME: May or may not include rhyme
REPETITION: The pattern and devices used for rhythmic and insistent repetition are up to the poet; this form is most poignant when spoken or chanted aloud

Aua

from MAGIC WORDS

To Lighten Heavy Loads

I speak with the mouth of Qeqertuanaq,
    and say:
I will walk with leg muscles strong as the
sinews on the shin of a little caribou calf.
I will walk with leg muscles strong as the
sinews on the shin of a little hare.
I will take care not to walk toward the dark.
I will walk toward the day.

———

Sir Charles G. D. Roberts
(1860–1943)

AUTOCHTHON

I

I am the spirit astir
    To swell the grain
When fruitful suns confer
    With labouring rain;
I am the life that thrills
    In branch and bloom;
I am the patience of abiding hills,
    The promise masked in doom.

II

When the sombre lands are wrung
    And storms are out,
And giant woods give tongue,
    I am the shout;
And when the earth would sleep,
    Wrapped in her snows,
I am the infinite gleam of eyes that keep
    The post of her repose.

III

I am the hush of calm,
    I am the speed,
The flood-tide's triumphing psalm,
    The marsh-pool's heed;
I work in the rocking roar
    Where cataracts fall;
I flash in the prismy fire that dances o'er
    The dew's ephemeral ball.

IV

I am the voice of wind
    And wave and tree,
Of stern desires and blind,
    Of strength to be;
I am the cry by night
    At point of dawn,
The summoning bugle from the unseen height,
    In cloud and doubt withdrawn.

V

I am the strife that shapes
    The stature of man,
The pang no hero escapes,
    The blessing, the ban;
I am the hammer that moulds
    The iron of our race,
The omen of God in our blood that a people beholds,
    The foreknowledge veiled in our face.

———————

Leonard Cohen
(b. 1934)

TWELVE O'CLOCK CHANT

Hold me hard light, soft light hold me,
Moonlight in your mountains fold me,
Sunlight in your tall waves scald me,
Ironlight in your wires shield me,
Deathlight in your darkness wield me.

In burlap bags the bankers sew me,
In countries far the merchants sell me,
In icy caves the princes throw me,
In golden rooms the doctors geld me,
In battlefields the hunters rule me.

I will starve till prophets find me
I will bleed till angels bind me,

Still I sing till churches blind me,
Still I love till cog-wheels wind me.

Hold me hard light, soft light hold me,
Moonlight in your mountains fold me,
Sunlight in your tall waves scald me,
Ironlight in your wires shield me,
Deathlight in your darkness wield me.

———————

Thuong Vuong-Riddick
(b. 1940)

MY BELOVED IS DEAD IN VIETNAM
For Trinh Cong Son, author of The Mad Woman

> *Dark or blue, all beloved, all beautiful.*
> *Numberless eyes have seen the day.*
> *They sleep in the grave,*
> *and the sun still rises.*
> — Sully Prudhomme

My beloved is
Dead in Diên Biên Phu
Dead in Lao Kay, dead in Cao Bang
Dead in Langson, dead in Mong Cai
Dead in Thai Nguyên, dead in Hanoï
Dead in Haïphong, dead in Phat Diêm
Dead in Ninh-Binh, dead in Thanh Hoa
Dead in Vinh, dead in Hatinh
Dead in Hue, dead in Danang, dead in Quang Tri

Dead in Quang Ngai, dead in Qui Nhon
Dead in Kontum, dead in Pleiku
Dead in Dalat, dead in Nha-Tranh
Dead in My Tho, dead in Tuy Hoa
Dead in Biên-Hoa, dead in Ban Me Thuot
Dead in Tayninh, dead in Anloc
Dead in Saigon, dead in Biên Hoa
Dead in Can Tho, dead in Soc Trang

Vietnam, how many times
I have wanted to call your name
I have forgotten
the human sound.

———————

Jon Furberg
(1944–1992)

NIGHTSPELL

Wounding words, whetted on flesh,
words of hooked steel, barbed hail,
sounds hooded and harmful

a word with a weapon in its hand,
a word that scars the air as it walks,
a word that wears a man's mask
word that flares and breaks,
word that blinds and disappears,
word that wakes and speaks,
                    eats, drinks, works, shits,
        fucks, sleeps, and dies!

word that shakes and falls because
no god appears though heart
cry out to very emptiness!
as if there once had been a better
birthingplace than rock
washed by cold waves and mother gone —
all-mothering sea, self-stirring,
pounding forever, self-forgetting.

"Let there be a spell tonight —
a nightspell fit to make men moan
and dream of starving, dream of flight
sleepless with shame, until I come,
till Dawn spread her slow, bright stream
along the low and waking land and say,
Behold your dead."

———

Penn Kemp
(b. 1944)

BIDDING SPELL

By Saturday cleanup.
By Sunday love feast.
By goodnight cuddles
        come back.

By your new bunk bed.
By rocketship plans.
By acting the hobbit
        come back.

By chinese checkers.
By your skill at chess.
By the lost game of Probe
       come back.

By skates. By skis.
By blue hockey cap
       come back.

By your moon in Capricorn.
By your Gemini rising.
By your sun in Leo
       come back.

By your shining face.
By your amazing inventions.
By your magic tricks
       come back.

By your folly.
By your fairness.
By your ancient soul
       come back.

By our sweet bond.
By the space we accord.
By the spirit we share
       come back.

By Aslan. By Superman.
By Gandalf. Come back
when you can.

bp Nichol
(1944–1988)

TURNIPS ARE

turnips are
inturps are
urnspit are
tinspur are
rustpin are
stunrip are
piturns are
ritpuns are
punstir are
nutrips are
suntrip are
untrips are
spinrut are
runspit are
pitnurs are
runtsip are
puntsir are
turnsip are
tipruns are
turpsin are
spurtin

Marilyn Bowering
(b. 1949)

WIDOW'S WINTER

Bless the red door open wide.
Bless the dead who play inside.

Call the waning, watchman moon,
as the baliff steps aside —

Christ, my heart's a bitter sinner,
rescue it from widow's winter.

———————

Brenda Brooks
(b. 1952)

LIFE, HAVING BECOME STILL

Pottery cup, broken handle,
lamp and wooden angel.
Bead of resin on leather thong,
window ledge, piece of amber.
Chamois pouch with pearl inside,
three almonds in a paper bag.
Bit of lava from cold volcano,
bed, sleep, long black candle.
Pencil shavings wrapped in a letter,
pottery cup, broken handle.

Theresa Kishkan
(b. 1955)

SPELL FOR A DAUGHTER

if I comb out my hair
and am careful
to compose it just so
on the pillow
bathe in two waters
remember the saints
out loud to the dark

if I hold him between
my thighs long enough
that nothing may spill
and we sleep thus

if I cover my head
in the face of the moon
plant nothing in this time
to take my attentions

if I tell no one her name
tell no one my hope
eat not of the flesh
of anything hooved

if I keep my arms free
and the small place inside

then she may come

Tim Bowling
(b. 1964)

MORENZ

The crowds, the cheers, the broken leg, the death.
The crowds, the tears, the open casket, the death.
The standings, the headlines, the copy-mad press.
The rushes, the goals, the sainthood in Quebec.

Ontario boy, la première étoile, Habitant captain.
O Canada in the Forum, O Canada in the Gardens.
The dekes, the grace, the wrists, the soft hands.
The masses, the headlines, the hearse, the fans.

Six Team League. The Roaring Twenties. Hat Trick.
The Stanley Cup, the records, the move, the check.
The break, the cast, the fever, the held breath.
The death, the death, the death, the death.

———————

Gregory Scofield
(b. 1966)

HIS FLUTE, MY EARS

piyis êkwa ê-tipiskâk êkwa
ôh, êkwa kâ-kimiwahk,
kâ-kimiwahk

earth smells, love medicine
seeping into my bones
and I knew
his wind voice
catching
the sleeping leaves

ôh, êkwa kâ-kimiwahk,
kâ-kimiwahk

I dreamed
him weaving spider threads
into my hair,
fingers of firefly
buzzing ears, the song
his flute
stealing clouds from my eyes

kâ-kimiwahk
I woke

numb in my bones.

piyis êkwa ê-tipiskâk êkwa
ôh, êkwa kâ-kimiwahk,
kâ-kimiwahk
At last it was night
oh, and it rained,
it rained

PALINDROME

A palindrome is commonly thought of as a word (e.g., "deified"), phrase or sentence (e.g., "Able was I ere I saw Elba") that reads alike both backward and forward. The word, derived from the Greek *palindromia*, literally means a running back again.

In poetry, the concept is expanded to multiple lines (or stanzas), where the lines in the first half of the poem are repeated, in reverse order, in the second half. As a poetic form, the palindrome appears to be quite new, and is just beginning to attract the attention of Canadian poets. To our knowledge, the first one published in Canada is Gudrun Wight's "The Gift Shop" (in a chapbook, *The Pender Island Poetry Anthology*[15]).

What lends the palindrome its power is the shift in emphasis or meaning when the lines are repeated, which allows the poet to give a different perspective in each half of the poem. For example, in Elizabeth Bachinsky's "ATM," what is "pink-cheeked and fussing for a nipple" is a baby in the first instance, and, poignantly, the husband in the second instance.

Bachinsky also changes nouns and/or pronouns to give her poem the turn she wants, using this variation to change the point of view from that of the wife in stanza one to that of the husband in stanza two. She also liberally shifts the ordering of phrases within lines on their second appearance, both to retain narrative sense and alter meaning in stanza two.

Another variation is Joe Denham's poem, which is divided into two sections ("Land" and "Sea"), each with five unrhymed couplets plus a final unrepeated line. Although they are outside the repetition pattern, those closing lines play a significant role in the poem, their insistent vowel and consonant sounds hissing in the surf like two waves, similar but not identical. The first, "… stone in the glare of the serpent-haired sun" ("Land") feels cast away, flotsam on the beach, stranded. The second, "floating in the

---

15 *Pender Island Poetry Anthology*, with a foreword by Roger Langrick, self published, Pender Island, 1990.

depths of dark, saline amnion" ("Sea") is allowed to sink, something lost or fading back into its original element; and we are irrevocably drawn back to the beginning of the poem, to "the littoral space between there and here."

Anne Simpson's "Mobius Strip," which visually depicts the poem's title by presenting ten couplets, each on its own page and straddling either side of a solid line, is a wonderful innovation that emphasizes the palindrome's flexibility.

THE TRADITIONAL FORM:

STANZAS:	Any number of stanzas of any length
METRE:	No set metre or syllable count required
RHYME:	No rhyme scheme required
REPETITION:	The ordering of the lines in the first half of the poem is reversed in the second half (and/or the ordering of words and even letters may be reversed in the two halves of the poem)

Fiona Tinwei Lam
(b. 1964)

LOOP

Soundlessly,
the woman is falling
from a mountain.
She leans
into a bed of wind.
Her eyes close —
a moment of deep rest.
A backdrop of clouds
tenderly pulls away.
She sinks so softly.
Her body still yearns to float
although it knows
the air isn't water. It ripples
through her hair and blue shirt
intimate and charged.
Second by second
the wind's hands releasing.
She comes through its muscle
in a world that tilts,
the forest a green smear,
her colours melting into landscape.
ambiguous and beautiful.

Ambiguous and beautiful,
her colours melting into landscape,
the forest, a green smear
in a world that tilts.
She comes through its muscle,
the wind's hands releasing
second by second
intimate and charged
through her hair and blue shirt.
The air isn't water — it ripples,
although it knows.
Her body still yearns to float.
She sinks so softly,
tenderly pulls away
a backdrop of clouds.
A moment of deep rest —
her eyes close
into a bed of wind.
She leans
from a mountain.
The woman is falling
soundlessly.

Anne Simpson
(b. 1956)

MÖBIUS STRIP

How it starts, how it ends: wild tuft in the sky, a cloud. This blue.

Floating. We take whatever shape we find. We learn each fold in air.

What we know best is what we want. Open palm of moon. Gone.

_____

Breath. The next and then. We've run out of a little clock of words.

Only this: one hand over another, our hearts folded like wings, sleep.

Small, smaller on a white bed. Each breath a country, a border. Love.

Waking. We could be envelopes or knives. Instead we're simple as cups:

———————————————————————————————————————

everything and nothing. Time is what we leave: your hands, your body ...

we're filled, yet we tip constantly. Goodbye. As for happiness —

---

it spills itself. The petal of a violet, a blue ear, listening. How easily

it spills itself. The petal of a violet, a blue ear, listening. How easily

---

we're filled, yet we tip constantly. Goodbye. As for happiness —

everything and nothing. Time is what we leave: your hands, your body …

Waking. We could be envelopes or knives. Instead we're simple as cups:

Small, smaller on a white bed. Each breath a country, a border. Love.

———

Only this: one hand over another, our hearts folded like wings, sleep.

Breath. The next and then. We've run out of a little clock of words.

What we know best is what we want. Open palm of moon. Gone.

Floating. We take whatever shape we find. We learn each fold in air.

How it starts, how it ends: a wild tuft in the sky, a cloud. This blue.

Julia Copus
(b. 1969)

THE BACK SEAT OF MY MOTHER'S CAR

We left before I had time
to comfort you, to tell you that we nearly touched
hands in that vacuous half-dark. I wanted
to stem the burning waters running over me like tiny
rivers down my face and legs, but at the same time I was reaching out
for the slit in the window where the sky streamed in,
cold as ether, and I could see your fat mole-fingers grasping
the dusty August air. I pressed my face to the glass;
I was calling you — Daddy! — as we screeched away into
the distance, my own hand tingling like an amputation.
You were mouthing something I still remember, the noiseless words
piercing me like that catgut shriek that flew up, furious as a sunset
pouring itself out against the sky. The ensuing silence
was the one clear thing I could decipher —
the roar of the engine drowning your voice,
with the cool slick glass between us.

With the cool slick glass between us,
the roar of the engine drowning, your voice
was the one clear thing I could decipher —
pouring itself out against the sky, the ensuing silence
piercing me like that catgut shriek that flew up, furious as a sunset.
You were mouthing something: I still remember the noiseless words,
the distance, my own hand tingling like an amputation.
I was calling to you, Daddy, as we screeched away into
the dusty August air. I pressed my face to the glass,
cold as ether, and I could see your fat mole-fingers grasping

for the slit in the window where the sky streamed in
rivers down my face and legs, but at the same time I was reaching out
to stem the burning waters running over me like tiny
hands in that vacuous half-dark. I wanted
to comfort you, to tell you that we nearly touched.
We left before I had time.

Sandy Shreve
(b. 1950)

DANCE

this is how the body can move
with grace and fortitude
remember them, two men
to the beat of one drum
their gymnastic limbs swinging
over and under, around
in the soft night air of a park
karate kicks just this far from skin
never come to blows
hands open into air
slow motion, a precision pose
anger transformed to the beautiful
in a dance

in a dance
anger transformed to the beautiful
slow motion, a precision pose
hands open into air
never come to blows
karate kicks just this far from skin
in the soft night air of a park
over and under, around
their gymnastic limbs swinging
to the beat of one drum
remember them, two men
with grace and fortitude
this is how the body can move

———————

Joe Denham
(b. 1975)

THE SHORELINE

I. Land

The littoral space between there and here
sings in the raking of wave over stone. Imagine

Hermaphroditus and Salmacis before Zeus split them:
this is the place where the harmonized voices of

sopranos and baritones become inseparable.
In the morning, clock radios air music

through twitching eyelids that open,
a trace of salt on tongues, then fall

back into the flux, dragging seaweed and sand
down with them. When they resurface, they'll turn

to stone in the glare of the serpent-haired sun.

II. Sea

Down with them. When they resurface, they'll turn
back into the flux, dragging seaweed and sand,

a trace of salt on tongues, then fall
through quivering eyelids that open …

In the morning, clock radios air music:
sopranos and baritones become inseparable.
This is the place where the harmonized voices of
Hermaphroditus and Salmacis, before Zeus split them,

sing in the raking of wave over stone. Imagine
the littoral space between there and here

floating in the depths of dark, saline amnion.

———————

Elizabeth Bachinsky
(b. 1976)

ATM

Her husband is a gentleman and, despite all, she loves him. His image
stays in her mind even when he is away in another country. She knows
he is important and that is why she doesn't pry into his affairs,
whether at home or away. There is no changing him, and besides
he is a good father. They are comfortable. Never have to confess their truth
to anyone other than themselves. They do as they like and
she likes it that way. Spends her days in her garden, no scrutiny there.
She dislikes scrutiny, being laid bare. Her family revealed only in photographs
arranged on the mantle at home, Christmas 1981, her youngest a baby then,
pink-cheeked and fussing for a nipple. So much has changed.
Far away in a country where her husband is a giant, still
broad as a table top, he shuffles into a glass booth, inserts a card into a slit
that spits bills into his palm. He is calm. He knows what he is.
What he has split apart he knows is forgiven.

What he has split apart he knows is forgiven.
He is calm. Spits bills into his palm. He knows what he is.
Broad as a table top, he shuffles into a glass booth, inserts a card into a slit
far away in a country where he is a giant, yet still
pink-cheeked and fussing for a nipple. So much has changed,
arranged on the mantle at home. Christmas 1981, his youngest a baby then.
His wife dislikes scrutiny, being laid bare. Her family revealed only in photographs.
She likes it that way. Spends her days in her garden, no scrutiny there
from anyone other than themselves. They do as they like and
he is a good father. They are comfortable. Never have to confess their truth
whether at home or away. There is no changing her, and besides
he is *important* and that is why she doesn't pry. Though his affairs
stay in her mind even when he is away in another country, she knows
her husband is a gentleman. Despite all, she loves him. His image.

PANTOUM

The pantoum is a French form that traditionally has any number of rhymed and metred four-line stanzas. But its most alluring feature is its intricate pattern of line repetition. Derived from the Malayan pantun[16], it was first used in France by Ernest Fouinet, and was popularized there by Victor Hugo and Charles Baudelaire in the 1800s.

Each line of a pantoum is used twice — lines 2 and 4 of the first stanza become lines 1 and 3 of the second, and so on until the last stanza. The final quatrain consists entirely of repeated lines: the first and third are the preceding stanza's lines 2 and 4; the second and fourth are the opening stanza's lines 3 and 1 in that order. So the poem circles back to its beginning, but with a deepened understanding.

The effect of the somersaulting lines can be delicate and hypnotic, as in Kirsten Emmott's "Labour Pantoum," or obsessive, as in Anita Lahey's "Post-War Procession." And, while at first glance it would seem the intense amount of repetition would work against extended narrative content, this assumption is belied in poems like Susan Elmslie's "Forecast: Nadja," where the story unfolds, shifting smoothly between past and present. Peter Garner's "Lucy, *Lucie*" reveals the pantoum's bilingual possibilities. And Lahey's poem shows the effect enjambed lines can have in this form — as when "... your head / inside the helmet ..." in stanza 3 shifts emphasis to "... this endless trudge / inside the helmet ..." in stanza 4.

One optional feature of the pantoum is to develop different themes in the first and second halves of each quatrain. Another option is to end with a couplet rather than the final quatrain described above (in which case, the final couplet consists of lines 3 and 1 of the opening stanza).

---

16 The pantun began as improvisational oral poetry, but by the fifteenth century it became part of Malaya's written literature (as a single rhymed syllabic quatrain). Robin Skelton, in *The Shapes of Our Singing*, says the first half makes "a statement which proves to be a metaphor for the statement made in the second, or which is the basis for an elaboration" (p. 235).

Poets often dispense with the rhyme and metre requirements of this form to focus entirely on the line repetition. Several of the poems included in this chapter fit into this category, including Emmott's and Elmslie's poems, and Marlene Cookshaw's "In the Spring of No Letters."

Another popular variation is to make changes in the repeated lines. Elmslie does this, often repeating only parts of lines or shifting their syntax to move the story forward. Maxianne Berger, in "Empty Chairs," subtly alters words to develop the sense of her poem. For instance, "She really misses her boyfriend" at the beginning becomes, at the end, "he" who "really wishes he had a boyfriend." Frequently, she rhymes a variation with the word it replaces (e.g., "misses" and "wishes" in the above), or makes a slight change to a word to come up with another (e.g., "debating" in line four loses its *eb* to become "dating" in line seven).

Poets will sometimes alter the repetition pattern at the end, closing with line 3 from stanza 1, rather than with the opening line. Richard Sanger's "Lines in the Sand" is an example of this variation.

THE TRADITIONAL FORM:

STANZAS: Any number of quatrains; may end in a couplet

METRE: Iambic tetrameter or iambic pentameter

RHYME: *abab*

REPETITION: • Lines 2 and 4 of each quatrain are repeated as lines 1 and 3 of the next, until the last stanza
            • Final stanza: all are repeated lines; in addition to maintaining the above pattern, lines 2 and 4 are the same as lines 3 and 1 of the first quatrain, so the poem ends as it begins
            • A four-stanza pantoum, for example, would use eight lines in the following pattern:
              1st: 1-2-3-4 **2nd**: 2-5-4-6 **3rd**: 5-7-6-8 **4th**: 7-3-8-1
            • If the above example closed with a couplet instead of a quatrain, it would end: **4th**: 3-1

Kirsten Emmott
(b. 1947)

LABOUR PANTOUM

are we there yet? are we there yet?
this is what it seems like
riding in the back seat of the car
that someone else is driving endlessly

this is what it seems like
sitting long hours by the labour bed
that someone else is driving endlessly
that her labour is bringing to inevitable birth

sitting long hours by the labour bed
with my hand on her brow or her swelling belly
that her labour is bringing to inevitable birth
while I, unimportant, look out the window

with my hand on her brow or her swelling belly
the trees and sky slide past
while I, unimportant, look out the window
and I daydream while it all goes by

the trees and sky slide past
as she lies back and rests, eyes closed
and I daydream while it all goes by
then she tenses and pants with a contraction

as she lies back and rests, eyes closed
we are silent in quiet expectation
then she tenses and pants with a contraction
we will be with her for as long as it takes

we are silent in quiet expectation
the night is long, day will soon break
we will be with her for as long as it takes
the city will turn pink with sunrise

the night is long, day will soon break
many babies are born at this hour
the city will turn pink with sunrise
the baby will turn pink with her first breath

many babies are born at this hour
eventually the baby will get to her destination
the baby will turn pink with her first breath
she will travel hopefully, having arrived

eventually the baby will get to her destination
like pulling into your driveway after days on the road
she will travel hopefully, having arrived
this is what it seems like

like pulling into your driveway after days on the road
days spent asking from the back seat —
this is what it seems like —
are we there yet? are we there yet?

———————

Lorna Crozier
(b. 1948)

THE DIRTY THIRTIES

Grandmother hoed her garden black and blue,
the sun shone without giving any light.
Fennel, basil, heartsease and rue,
she seeded snow to heal a season's blight.

The sun shone without giving any light
and cows pulled their calves back to the womb.
No snow could heal the years' sad blight.
A boy played the bones in the upstairs room.

The cow pulled the calf inside her womb.
No milk from a stone, the old woman said.
My dad played the bones in his attic room
where mice ran on wires above his head.

No blood from a stone, the old woman said.
Or snow from snow, or sorrow from a pin.
Mice chewed the wires above their heads
and all things seemed grey and poorer then.

No snow from snow or sorrow from a pin.
Fennel from basil, heartsease from common rue.
All things seemed older and harder then
when Grandma beat her garden black and blue.

Maxianne Berger
(b. 1949)

EMPTY CHAIRS

She really misses her boyfriend
some mornings sitting alone
with coffee in her dark kitchen
debating what she might've done.

The same mornings he sits alone
and wonders why he's so depressed
dating; what he might've done
also to get a pick-up for sex.

She wonders why she's so depressed
without this man — her mind astir
also at what he'd pick up from sex –
face to face with his empty chair.

Without any man in mind, stirring
his coffee in the dark kitchen
he faces a faceless empty chair,
    really wishes he had a boyfriend.

Marlene Cookshaw
(b. 1953)

IN THE SPRING OF NO LETTERS

Do I think of you often, my husband wants to know.
I lie and say no or lie and say yes.
I do not think of you, exactly.
My body has words with your ghost sometimes.

I lie and say no, or lie and say yes.
We are never upright when the truth is spoken.
My body has words with your ghost sometimes.
We speak in tongues, a lingual exchange.

We are never upright when the truth is spoken.
I am used up by what the body cannot parse.
We speak in tongues, a lingual exchange
I understand and do not at the same time.

I am used up by what the body cannot parse.
The sauna stove next door's alight again.
I understand this and do not at the same time.
Is time the issue? How many times, he asks.

Next door the sauna stove's alight again.
I know, for instance, from the smoke that it is evening.
Is time the issue? How many times he asks,
as if day were a pie: proportional, divisible, dessert.

For instance, from the smoke, I know it's evening.
I'm baking yams. The dog's content.
And day's a pie: proportional, divisible, dessert.
The smoke rises like a finer form of blossom.

I'm baking yams. The dog's content.
I do not think of you exactly.
The smoke rises like a finer form of blossom.
Do I think of you? My husband wants to know.

———————

Richard Sanger
(b. 1960)

LINES IN THE SAND

Mother, you never said it wasn't true.
I ate a plate of snakes for dinner
While the choirboys recited all they knew
And outside they clobbered some poor sinner.

I ate a plate of snakes for dinner
Drank arak, cleared my throat and smacked my lips
And outside they clobbered some poor sinner,
Some poor bastard who, caught in the eclipse,

Drank arak, cleared his throat and smacked his lips
As if he thought his friends were still on top —
Those poor bastards who, caught in the eclipse,
Would see their whole country turn to dust, and stop.

As if I thought our friends were still on top.
Mother, you never said it wasn't true.
I saw a whole country turn to dust, and stop,
While the choirboys recited all they knew.

Peter Garner
(b. 1965)

LUCY, *LUCIE*

In 1974, Donald Johanson discovered a near-complete female hominid skeleton near Hadar, Ethiopia. *On trouvera, un jour lointain, sur une autre route montagneuse, les restes d'une femme qui aura perdu le contrôle de son véhicule.*

three million years later, they found her
tire marks leading to the edge of a gully
sur un coteau, une côte et un os pelvien se trouvent
en bas, une nouvelle Grand Prix, renversée

des traces de pneus mènent au bord du ravin
la fumée monte, se mêle avec la brume
below, a grand new prize is overturned
a wheel, spinning slowly, seeks the road

rising into the mist, smoke mingles
the radio plays a Beatles song
lentement, une roue tourne, cherchant la route
sans nom: on l'appellera « Lucie »

la radio chante une chanson des Beatles
elle marche maintenant la tête haute
she has no name — let's call her "Lucy"
she had no past, but she will have a future

walking now with head held high
on a hillside, a rib, a pelvic bone lay there
elle n'avait pas de passé, mais elle aura un futur
dans trois millions d'années, ils la trouveront

Susan Elmslie
(b. 1968)

FORECAST: NADJA

"I knew everything, so hard have I tried to read in my streams of tears."
— Nadja

"The essential thing is that I do not suppose there can be much difference for Nadja between the inside of a sanitarium and the outside."
— André Breton, *Nadja*

Flowers drown when the ground gets sodden.
I knew everything, so hard have I tried
to notice things,
to read in my streams of tears.

I knew everything, so hard.
Fingers thrumming, nails chewed down,
I tried to read in my streams of tears
the prognosis, the weather report. More rain:

fingers thrumming, nails. Down
water and pills.
The prognosis, the weather report? More rain
apparently. That's what I can expect:

water and pills.
Storm clouds drop like a dressing gown.
Apparently, that's what I can expect.
And then after a time the weather clears.

Storm clouds drop like a dressing gown
again. Months later I visit the garden.
For a time, the weather's clear.
So delicate I scarcely touch the ground.

Again, months later, I visit the garden:
mayflies braid the air
so delicate I scarcely touch the ground,
like girls skipping double Dutch,

mayflies braiding the air.
And for now I feel good in my skin
like girls skipping double Dutch
one, two, beside my slatted wood bench.

And for now I feel good in my skin.
The girls are singing
three, four, beside my slatted wood bench
something luminous, the beginning of the word hope.

The girls are singing,
Rain, rain, go away, come again another day, and
something luminous, the beginning of the word hope
is folded with their skipping ropes.

Rain's come again, rain another day.
At the Sainte-Anne, I'm put away.
Hopes furl like the skipping ropes,
like umbrellas in the lost and found.

At the Sainte-Anne, I'm put away.
Who could distinguish me from the other
umbrellas in the lost and found?
The nurses kindly take me out for air.

Who could distinguish me from the others
shuffling along the tree-lined Allée Paul Verlaine,
inmates the kindly nurses take outside for the air
darkening slatted benches under the linden trees?

Lines from Verlaine I've always loved
repeat my pain, like the rain
darkening slatted benches under the linden trees:
il pleure dans mon coeur comme il pleut sur la ville.

The rain repeats my pain, like
the grating sound of a key turning in a lock.
O bruit doux de la pluie par terre et sur les toits!
In a week I'm moved to the Perray-Vaucluse.

The grating sound of a key turning in a lock,
the wretched view of the garden —
the week I'm moved to the Vaucluse
I begin to know everything.

The wretched view of the garden.
The stone wall, gatehouse, regimen.
I begin to know everything:
the difference between the inside of a sanatorium

and the outside of a sanatorium.
When I'm clear they let me stroll the grounds.
When I'm threatening rain, they lock me in again.
Somebody turns the water on and off.

When I'm clear they let me stroll the grounds
to notice things. Long walks in the rain make me
so muddy the bath water turns brown.
Flowers drown.

———————

Anita Lahey
(b. 1972)

POST-WAR PROCESSION
after "Infantry, near Nijmegan, Holland, 1946"
(Alex Colville, oil on canvas)

Envy the barrel's ability to contain nothing.
You stink of blood, a blown-open field, severed
limbs. The march in was less pungent. Puddles, open
wounds along the ditch. Your rifle cools your neck.

You stink of blood, a blown-open field. Severed,
still following orders, boots of the men in front,
wounds along the ditch. Your rifle, your neck.
The yellow leak of sky. Bodies reek in your head.

Still following orders. Boots of the men in front
reflect your own: polished, tightly tied.
That yellow leak of sky. Bodies reek. Your head
inside the helmet; gripping your skull.

Reflect. Your own polished, tightly tied
meltdown. Mud. This endless trudge
inside the helmet gripping your skull.
The march continues. On the other side:

meltdown, mud, this endless trudge —
hands unfolding letters you barely wrote.
The march continues on the other side.
The horizon claws you back with white fingers,

hands unfolding. Letters you barely wrote
wish your work is done. Forget glory being alive.
The horizon claws you back; its white fingers
needle your every accomplishment, ghastly

wish. Your work is done. Forget glory: being alive
is the long walk you knew it would be,
needing your every ghastly accomplishment.
Envy the barrel's ability. Contain nothing.

RONDEAU FAMILY

P oems in the rondeau family are all distinguished by their use of refrains and just two rhymes. Those included in this chapter are the rondeau, roundel, rondeau redoubled (or redoublé) and rondel.

The term rondeau originally referred to all French fixed forms that included refrains of any sort. And over the years the term roundel has sometimes been used as a synonym for the rondeau and the rondel. All of this can get a bit confusing — but in fact, while these forms have similarities, each has its own distinct features.

The rondeau emerged as a form in its own right by the fifteenth century. A poem with three stanzas of five, four and six lines, it has just two rhymes and one, unrhymed, refrain. The refrain is the first part of line one, repeated at the end of stanzas two and three. The other lines usually have eight or ten syllables each, rhyming *aabba* in the first and third stanzas and *aab* in the second. John McCrae's "In Flanders Fields" is one of the best known rondeaux. Marilyn Bowering's "Autobiography" varies the form, with loosely metered lines and a refrain that becomes part, rather than all, of the closing lines in stanzas two and three.

English poet Charles Swinburne developed the roundel as a variation of the rondeau. His version, too, is divided into three stanzas, but these are shorter — four, three and four lines. He uses the first part of line one as a refrain, but departs from the French form by repeating it at the end of stanzas one and three only. The other differences are that, throughout, he laces the two rhymes (e.g., *aba bab aba*) and requires no set metre or syllable count. Colin Morton follows the form closely, with a refrain of "In this empty room," but compresses the eleven lines into two stanzas.

The rondeau redoubled, another version of the rondeau, has six stanzas — five quatrains and a closing quintet. (The quatrains resemble a glosa in that the first quatrain provides the last line for each of the next four.) Like the rondeau, this poem ends as it begins, i.e., with the first half of the initial quatrain's opening line. The stanzas alternate between two rhyme schemes, *abab* and *baba*, and normally all lines except the last have a common metre or syllable count. Margaret Avison, in "Rondeau Redoublé," shortens the form to five stanzas — four quatrains and a quintet.

The rondel is a thirteen- or fourteen-line poem, usually divided into three stanzas — two quatrains and either a quintet or a sestet. The first two lines of stanza one reappear as refrains at the end of stanzas two and three (the final line is optional). While the form requires no set metre or syllable count, often poets keep all lines to either eight or ten syllables. Émile Nelligan's "Roundel to my Pipe" is actually a thirteen-line rondel of eight syllable lines and a somewhat varied rhyme scheme. Nelligan's poem (in this translation) keeps to the usual pattern, *abba*, in the first four lines, but varies the next eight lines, using *baab baab* instead of *abab abba*. The triolet (see Triolet chapter) was an early form of the rondel.

More flexible is the roundelay, which requires only the use of a refrain. Poets, however, are extremely creative in their application of this element, often varying it or using additional repetition devices to intensify a poem's effect. For example, Dennis Lee in "On A Kazoo" uses different line breaks each time he repeats the chorus, "singin / high / on a wire all / day. / Hey!" Irving Layton in "Song for Naomi" varies his refrain line slightly ("My lovely daughter," "My foolish daughter," "My little daughter," etc.) and also repeats single words almost immediately, but in a slightly different form (e.g. "tall / Are taller," "fast / And faster").

THE TRADITIONAL FORM:

Rondeau

STANZAS: Three stanzas: the first is a quintet; the second, a quatrain; and the third, a sestet

METRE: Usually 8 or 10 syllables in each line, except for the short-ened refrain lines

RHYME: *aabba / aab*R / *aabba*R (R stands for the refrain)

REPETITION: The refrain is the first phrase of line 1, repeated as the last line in both the quatrain and the sestet; the refrain is outside the rhyme scheme

Roundel

STANZAS: Three stanzas: the first is a quatrain; the second, a tercet; and the third, a quatrain

METRE: No set metre or syllable count required

RHYME: *aba*R / *bab* / *aba*R (R stands for the refrain)

REPETITION: The refrain is the first part of line 1, which is repeated as lines 4 and 11 (R may rhyme with line 2, but this is optional)

Rondeau redoubled

STANZAS: Six stanzas; the first five are quatrains and the sixth is a quintet

METRE: All lines, except for the final shortened refrain, have a common metre or syllable count (the pattern is up to the poet)

RHYME: $A^1B^1A^2B^2$ / *bab*A^1 / *aba*B^1 / *bab*A^2 / *aba*B^2 / *baba*R (capitals stand for repeated lines and R stands for the repeated half line; numbered capitals, i.e., A^1B^1 represent rhymed, but otherwise different refrain lines)

REPETITION: Five refrains, each repeated once; the first quatrain provides the fourth line for each of the next four stanzas; the first part of line 1 is line 5 of the last stanza (and is thus outside the *ab* rhyme scheme)

Rondel

STANZAS: Three stanzas; the first two are quatrains and the third can be either a quintet or sestet

METRE: No set metre or syllable count required, though often the lines are all 8 or 10 syllables each

RHYME: *ABba* / *abAB* / *abbaA(B)* (capitals stand for refrains)

REPETITION: Two refrains: the first is line 1, repeated as lines 7 and 13; the second is line 2, repeated as lines 8 and 14 (line 14 is optional)

Roundelay

The only requirement is the use of a regularly repeated line or stanza.

John McCrae
(1872–1918)

IN FLANDERS FIELDS

In Flanders fields the poppies blow
Between the crosses, row on row,
    That mark our place; and in the sky
    The larks, still bravely singing, fly
Scarce heard amid the guns below.

We are the Dead. Short days ago
We lived, felt dawn, saw sunset glow,
    Loved and were loved, and now we lie
        In Flanders fields.

Take up our quarrel with the foe:
To you from failing hands we throw
    The torch; be yours to hold it high.
    If ye break faith with us who die
We shall not sleep, though poppies grow
        In Flanders fields.

Émile Nelligan
(1879–1941)

ROUNDEL TO MY PIPE
(translated by P.F. Widdows)

Feet on the fender by firelight,
With glass in hand, good pipe, content,
Let's keep our friendly precedent
And dream alone, this winter night.

Since heaven has grown so virulent,
(As though my troubles were too slight!)
Feet on the fender by firelight,
With glass in hand, let's dream, content.

Soon death, by my presentiment,
Will drag me from this hellish site
To good old Lucifer's; all right!
We'll smoke in that establishment,

Feet on the fender, by firelight.

Irving Layton
(b. 1912)

SONG FOR NAOMI

Who is that in the tall grasses singing
By herself, near the water?
I can not see her
But can it be her
Than whom the grasses so tall
Are taller,
My daughter,
My lovely daughter?

Who is that in the tall grasses running
Beside her, near the water?
She can not see there
Time that pursued her
In the deep grasses so fast
And faster
And caught her,
My foolish daughter.

What is the wind in the fair grass saying
Like a verse, near the water?
Saviours that over
All things have power
Make Time himself grow kind
And kinder
That sought her,
My little daughter.

Who is that at the close of the summer
Near the deep lake? Who wrought her
Comely and slender?
Time but attends and befriends her
Than whom the grasses though tall
Are not taller,
My daughter,
My gentle daughter.

———————

Margaret Avison
(b. 1918)

RONDEAU REDOUBLÉ

Along the endless avenue stand poles.
Divorced from origin, their end's obscure.
There are doors lined up all along these walls.
Some open by the clock, and some immure

No sick child gazing out, but furniture
For dentists, typists, or those crooked halls
To empty lofts lost countrymen endure.
Along the endless avenue stand poles.

Under the negro sun the full tide rolls.
Crowds straggle gradually. There are fewer
By 3 p.m. (with these a pigeon strolls).
Divorced from origin, their end's obscure.

Dark brings the estuary, no vein pure
Enough to bleed freely. Horizon's holes
Fill slowly. Lights. Night's for the amateur.
There are doors lined up all along these walls.

Neons blaze lonelier. The foghorn bawls.
Taxis are knowledgeable now, and sure.
The wary one eyes EXIT. It appals.
(Some open by the clock and some immure
Along the endless avenue).

Dennis Lee
(b. 1939)

ON A KAZOO

Wal   I got a gal
         on my   kazoo
    and she looks real good,
like a good gal
              should,
                      singin
              high
on a wire all
              day.

         Hey!

        I got a fly
in my   little eye
        an it's buzzin right around
till I seen that
                sound,
        singin
                high on a
                        wire all
                                day.

        Hey!

                I
                        got a
        lady
                an a
        lady got me: an I'm
gonna play around
                        with her *sweet right*
                knee!
        singin
                high on a wire all day.
                                Hey!
                Stay
        high on a wire all day!

————————

Colin Morton
(b. 1948)

from THREE SMALL ROOMS

In this empty room we gather
The reports of all the blind men
Without asking how or whether
In this empty room
These tales of snake or tree or fan
Can be reconciled together.

We mix guesses, lies and half-lies, then
From the ludicrous palaver
Try to sort out truth from lie again
And start the conjuring over
In this empty room.

———————

Marilyn Bowering
(b. 1949)

from AUTOBIOGRAPHY

4

I would have wept if weeping
netted continents in heart's safekeeping:
what do you want, why call or write
to me? My heart's closed, it's night,
my hand will never trace your cheek in sleeping.

As dawn began its walk, its sweep
of all good sense, you took my hand: fleeting
touch that left its mark — I feel it yet — why should I fight
to lie to you? I would have wept.

There are no words for this regret, a leaking
hard, dry as drought, unstaunched by all these months: needing
you is all it is, a wound against myself, slight
as a sting of frost or second-sight —
I have no heart for change, no grieving (understand?) —
But, oh, I could have wept.

Mark Abley
(b. 1955)

DOWN

These are the trees chopped down, chopped in a day.
The mahogany stretches from here to St. Eustache.
Teak sprawls even farther in the opposite direction.
Oaks are jostling ginkgos, figs rub up against maples,
date palms disturb the highways; the birchbark is white trash.
These are the trees chopped down, chopped in a day.

These are the trees chopped down, chopped in the night.
I never thought so many walnut logs could fit on the back
of a truck. Now nothing surprises me: not the littered olives,
not the stink of eucalyptus, not even the crumpled
mountains of bamboo. Something lived in a snarl of sumac.
These are the trees chopped down, chopped in the night.

These are the trees chopped down, chopped by the hour.
Tomorrow they'll emerge as plywood, pulp or fire.
A lifetime ago last week they sheltered rainbows in a canopy
or tangled against snow, subarctic bonsai:
willow, larch, arbutus, the chainsawed fruits of desire.
These are the trees chopped down, chopped by the hour.

SESTINA

The sestina was invented in medieval Provence by the troubadour Arnaut Daniel.[17] In *The Making of a Poem*, editors Mark Strand and Eavan Boland note that the troubadours often competed with one another to create "the wittiest, most elaborate, most difficult styles" and that the sestina "was the form for a master troubadour." It consists of six unrhymed stanzas of six lines each, followed by a concluding three-line envoy, and features an intriguing pattern of word repetition. Although rare, the poet may also use a metered line, as in Fred Cogswell's "The Edge" ("A <u>swish</u>ing <u>noise</u> from <u>just</u> be<u>hind</u> my <u>head</u>").

The delight and challenge of the sestina is that the words that end each of the six lines in stanza one must be repeated in a particular order as the end words of each of the following stanzas. The envoy also contains all six of the repeated words, two in each line, again in a particular order. There was probably once a magical significance to this order, but if so, it appears to have been lost.

The *New Princeton Encyclopedia of Poetry and Poetics* cites the Comte de Gramont, who was responsible for the revival of the sestina in France in the nineteenth century, describing this form as "a reverie in which the same ideas, the same objects, occur to the mind in a succession of different aspects, which nonetheless resemble one another, fluid and changing shape like the clouds in the sky." The invitation to the poet is to keep the clouds moving — to divert the reader from the pervasive presence of the final six words.

This is done in a variety of ways. Rachel Rose enjambs the lines in "The Geographic Tongue" ("the village river drifted / over my grandmother's bare feet") and Cogswell uses words that sound the same but have different meanings and spellings ("I" / "eye"). Sue Wheeler, in "In Juarez," uses

---

17 Ron Padget, in *The Teachers & Writers Handbook of Poetic Forms*, comments that, "The troubadours were travelling French poet-musicians, some of them noblemen or crusader-knights, who flourished from the end of the eleventh century through the thirteenth century. The female counterparts of the troubadors were called trobairitiz" (p. 175).

translations and close forms of the Mexican word "Cucaracha," ("cock-roaches," "brooches," "roaches," "reaches" and "breaches"). Variety (and diversion) can also be found in her use of inclusive/compound words such as "olive," "alive," "live."

In "Ritual," Sue Chenette introduces yet another way to vary the form with what she calls "a disguised sestina." Instead of end words, she uses end categories: tree or tree part, earth, water, creature, body part, and grassy plant[18]. So, for example, the "tree or tree part" becomes "sapling," "maple's crown," "shoots," "leaves," "roots" and "tree." And Jay Macpherson, departing even further from the form, surprises and delights us with her unique approach to the repeated end words in "The Beauty of Job's Daughters."

The sestina is well suited to writing about obsession. Bruce Meyer uses this feverish quality in "The Lovers' Sestina," where the very short lines and incessantly repeating words emphasize the obsessions of a lover. The weaving in and out, back and forth of the six words can create, as in Al Purdy's "Sestina on a Train," a net in which the reader is caught and from which s/he may run, only to discover — by the time the envoy snaps the net shut — there is no escape.

THE TRADITIONAL FORM:

STANZA:	Six six-line stanzas with a concluding three-line envoy
METRE:	Rare but may be metred
RHYME:	None required; word repetition replaces a rhyme scheme
REPETITION:	• The concluding words of each line in stanza 1 are repeated in a set pattern; if the numbers 1, 2, 3, 4, 5, 6 represent the end words in stanza 1, then the repetition pattern in the next five stanzas is: 6-1-5-2-4-3 / 3-6-4-1-2-5 / 5-3-2-6-1-4 / 4-5-1-3-6-2 / 2-4-6-5-3-1
	• In the envoy, the pattern is 2-5 / 4-3 / 6-1 (where 2, 4, and 6 are used mid-line and 5, 3, 1 are used at line ends)

---

18   In correspondence with the editors.

Fred Cogswell
(1917–2004)

THE EDGE

The old fear of the dark has not returned
For fifty years. It perished the last year
Of my boyhood one evening when I
Heard — hunting for moths at the woodland edge —
A swishing noise from just behind my head
And fled through moonlit fields with panic speed.

I could not outrun it. Despite my speed
The thing I heard grew louder till I turned
Suddenly and my straw hat fell off my head.
I realized then the fearful sound my ear
Had caught was merely that hat's broad-brimmed edge
On my shoulders. The monster? It was I.

And then beneath the moon's sardonic eye
I homeward sauntered at a decent speed,
Knowing at last where the nerve-prickling edge
Of my terror lay. It was I who'd turned
The dark into a nightmare land of fear
And the real *loup-garou* was in my head.

With fear of darkness went the very head
And heart of my intimate delight. I
No longer found the quest for moths a dear
And sharp enjoyment as I bade God-speed
To the relief that came when horrors turned
Out to be moth wings at the wood's dark edge.

Perhaps I simplify, but still the edge
Where fear and hope meet — whether in the head
Or not — is the one space on which are turned
Most masterworks, though dread for sanity
Impels us with worldly wisdom's speed
To change heaven and hell for a safer sphere.

Today I mourn the conquest of my fear
Even as my life slips closer to the ledge
From which one day this routine self will speed
I know not where. I wish that to my head
That wild boy's madness had again returned
To conjure phantoms in the night's dark eye.

As boy, I turned my head from hope and fear.
Now, safe too long, I cannot find the edge
Where the wolf-eyes gleam and frail moth wings speed.

Al Purdy
(1918–2000)

SESTINA ON A TRAIN

I've always been going somewhere — Vancouver
or old age or somewhere ever since I can remember:
and this woman leaning over me, this madwoman
while I was sleeping, whispering, "Do you take drugs?"
And the sight of her yellow-white teeth biting
the dark open wide and white eyes like marbles

children play with but no children play with marbles
like those — saying, "Do you take drugs?" And Vancouver
must be somewhere near this midnight I can't remember
where tho only the sister holding the madwoman,
fighting her: me saying stupidly, "No, no drugs."
She wanting to talk and sitting there biting

at something I couldn't see what the hell she was biting,
only her white eyes like aching terrible marbles
and mouth crying out, "I don't want to go to Vancouver!
Don't let them take me!" She didn't remember
the sad scared children, children of the madwoman
herself, recognized only me the stranger, asking what drugs

I took and wouldn't stop asking that. What such drugs
do besides closing those eyes and keeping those teeth from biting
that tongue into rags and soothing a forehead damp as marble's
cold stone couldn't be altogether bad eh? All the way to Vancouver
where I was going and thought I could remember
having lived once I comforted the madwoman

while the sister minded her frightened children: madwoman,
courtesan, mother, wife, in that order. Such drugs
as I know of don't cause this snapping and biting
at shadows or eyes like glaring lacustral marbles
and mouth crying, "Don't let them take me to Vancouver!"
And leaning her head on my shoulder's scared calm ... I remember

now the promise I made and do not wish to remember
going somewhere and falling asleep on the train and the madwoman
shakes me softly awake again and, "Yes, I do take drugs,"
I say to her and myself: "I get high on hemp and peyote biting
at scraps of existence I've lost all the smoky limitless marbles
I found in my life once lost long before Vancouver —"

I've forgotten that child, his frantic scratching and biting
for something he wanted and lost — but it wasn't marbles.
I remember the Mountie waiting, then the conductor's "Vancouver next!
  Vancouver!"

Jay Macpherson
(b. 1931)

THE BEAUTY OF JOB'S DAUGHTERS

The old, the mad, the blind have fairest daughters.
Take Job: the beasts the accuser sends at evening
Shoulder his house and shake it; he's not there,
Attained in age to inwardness of daughters,
In all the land no women found so fair.

Angels and sons of God are nearest neighbours,
And even the accuser may repair
To walk with Job in pleasures of his daughters:
Wide shining rooms more warmly lit at evening,
Gardens beyond whose secrets scent the air.

Not wiles of men nor envy of the neighbours,
Riches of earth, nor what heaven holds more rare,
Can take from Job the beauty of his daughters,
The gardens in the rock, music at evening,
And cup so full that all who come must share.

Perhaps we passed them? it was late, or evening,
And surely those were desert stumps, not daughters,
In fact we doubt that they were ever there.
The old, the mad, the blind have fairest daughters.
In all the land no women found so fair.

Sue Chenette
(b. 1942)

RITUAL

All summer I've watered your maple sapling,
spindly bole in a new-mounded collar of earth.
I plant puddled footprints at the river's edge,
squat to fill a bucket, scatter minnows
with my small commotion, then, arm out for balance,
tramp up the bank through brush and waist-high grasses.

In the sunny back and forth a stem of purple loosestrife
might catch my thought... or the maple's crown
bent toward the river. Grasses mat under my feet.
At the tree's base I tilt the bucket and watch soil
darken, each time a wider ring. Dog-walkers
pass on the path, mallards on the slow current.

Seven years since you died. You walked by this river
in your good times, when you visited, scanned the weeds
for muskrats. Once you saw a great blue heron.
Even when darkness branched in you, pushed shoots
into each thought, you were eased seeing an oak in a field,
clouds of birds settled with beating wings.

Belatedly I've chosen a memorial, this tree, muscled
into spring ground by a city crew. *Soak it,*
they said, *enough so water stands in the dirt saucer.*
I hadn't counted on that — weekly ritual of reeds
and river, lift or droop of leaves.
Once, the current I stirred drew a crayfish

from under its rock. I remembered my brother saw a beetle
and knew it was you, visiting, with an iridescent green back.
I couldn't accept such solace, your death like twisted roots
still buried in me, closed off, tears sealed up
with questions that spiral and cling like bindweed.
I didn't ask them, as I crossed the hard ground

between river and maple in fresh-dug sod.
But I've felt an ease in my physical self,
something soothed in hours among wild phlox
and alder brush that left fine scratches on my knees
while my arm grew stronger with the sloshing pail,
a ring of grass greened round your tree.

I think you'd like the fall colors across the river —
and that crayfish that scutters in the rocks and mud —
here, where, pail in hand, I've worn a grassy path.

———————

Sue Wheeler

(b. 1942)

IN JUAREZ

This is the girl's first nightclub, in Juarez.
Kids can get in anywhere in border
towns, the trinketed streets and make-you-sick water.
Wide-hat musicians blare "La Cucaracha."
The father buys the girl a Shirley Temple and aims
his gin-soaked toothpick at an olive.

This afternoon they passed alleys alive
with rats and the souvenirs of Juarez,
hands slapping tortillas and hands held out for alms,
the gold cloth, a saint's knuckle stitched in its border
where anyone can kiss it, cockroaches,
bandits, and do the local people drink the water?

Fault of the Pope. That's what her
father says. The band cranks it up for the live
floor show, sequins and shimmying brooches.
The marquee said "Bestest dancers de Juarez!"
a fraction the price of shows across the border,
and look! — one is the girl's double, there, by the potted palms.

Rhinestones river her look-alike arms.
Her hairdo is the very same ducktail, slicked with water.
Same smile, eyes, colour. (Everyone is brown this side the border.)
If the girl learned Spanish could she live
here? Would she fit right in, in Juarez,
ignoring for the moment the roaches?

She stares and wonders. The music reaches
its climax — maracas, a windmill of arms.
The father, who looks a little like the hero Benito Juarez,
holds his hand up to call the waiter.
The twin's bare back cha-chas toward the rest of her life.
In childish Spanish, the father gives his order.

A dried-up riverbed patrols the border.
Rifles and chainlink, uncountable breaches.
Are there, then, a number of possible lives?
Holes in the expected, like magic charms?
Whisha-whish go the dusty palms. *Answers are water.*
The girl sips the night-sugar taste of Juarez.

Dinner arrives on the arms of the waiter.
The father reaches for his *cabrito*, specialty of Juarez.
Life, whispers the sweating glass at the drink's sweet border.

———

Bruce Meyer
(b. 1957)

THE LOVERS' SESTINA

Am I
this song
celebrating you,
each drawn
breath praising
the world?

The world
that I
know, praising
with song,
is drawn
loving you.

Are you
the world
completely drawn,
all I
am, song
for praising?

This praising
that you
call song
is world
enough. I
am drawn,

slowly drawn
to praising
what I
love: you,
the world,
becoming song,

simple song
simply drawn,
a world
where praising
canticles you,
declaring I

am alive, a song of you
drawn from praising
all I know of the world.

Rachel Rose
(b. 1970)

SESTINA OF THE GEOGRAPHIC TONGUE

Geographic Tongue:

*"One with raised areas due to the thickening of the surface cells, giving the
appearance of a map."* — The New American Medical Dictionary

*"… outlined by margins in a grey-yellow or whitish, constantly changing pattern.
Also known as fissured tongue, lingua plicata, or migratory glossitis."*
— Dictionary of Medical Syndromes

If I offered you my geographic tongue,
would you be able to tell without speaking:
This is a road map. This is a map home.
Here is where the village river drifted
over my grandmother's bare feet. Here is her street
where the wind dropped bone grit in the throat. Here is the star

with its six points, and here are the stars
sharpening their points against many tongues.
Some drank starlight on these barbed streets.
Some ate grit and clay and died without speaking.
Those who survived were cut loose and drifted
through a strange geography, far from home

and familiar tongues. No, Montreal was never home
to her, just a place to pass dreams to her children: *star
light, star bright*, and their English was a drift
of snow in the mouth that froze her tongue
and split her apart from them. She made them speak
her errands and was afraid to go alone in the street.

Now my tongue is cobbled like a village street
and the river of her girlhood has finally come home
to sing in my mouth. I know, though my father rarely spoke
of it. I know about the spoiled meat torn like a bloody star
between the village children who died of eating, numb-tongued,
mute. The starlit worksongs that drifted

over the Hungarian fields all the way to Israel, drifted
like a red tide of song, in and out of the oily streets.
Here is her only son speaking a once-dead tongue
and here are the blue-skinned grapes of his new home.
Here are the hops. The same low stars
hang over the kibbutz. Here is her son standing without speaking

and becoming my father. Without speaking
I want you to understand. I am proof of my parents' drifting
love. I am proof of the shawl and the star
that those left behind wore like a caul and a scar through streets
bound in wire. Her memories of home
became a burnt map, a gutted flame, and many tongues

were cut out for speaking. And the streets
were darkened by drifting ash and home
now is just the faint lines of a star etched upon my tongue.

SONNET

Jorge Luis Borges has said, "there is something mysterious about the sonnet,"[19] and perhaps there is no more logical explanation for this form's power and longevity. The sonnet was created early in the thirteenth century by Giacomo da Lentino in the court of Emperor Frederick II in Sicily. Based on a Sicilian folk song, the name derives from the Italian, *sonetto*, for "little sound" or "song."

The Italian sonnet was a revolutionary form, written in the popular local language (Italian rather than Latin) and intended for individual silent reading rather than public performance. It was carefully structured; the opening eight lines presented and developed a dilemma and then there was a turn, a space, sometimes imaginary and sometimes represented by a blank line, in which something was resolved. The closing six-line stanza then stated the resolution of the problem.

In his book *The Birth of the Modern Mind: Self, Consciousness, and the Invention of the Sonnet*, Paul Oppenheimer concludes that the sonnet was the first lyric form of "self-consciousness." In a sonnet, then, writers — and readers — were, for the first time in European poetry, encouraged to think for themselves.

There was another bonus. Until this time in Europe, under the code of courtly love, the dominant French troubadour-style of poetry (strictly for the upper classes) consisted of lyrics that allowed a man (but rarely women) to praise, but not to persuade, a lover. The sonnet offered a solution to both exclusions. Here was a poem of only fourteen lines that was persuasive, emotionally charged, and that could easily be slipped into a waiting hand. Not only were women among the earliest writers of sonnets, but the form encouraged both women and men of all stations to communicate directly

---

19 Borges, in Edward Hirsch, *How to Read a Poem and Fall in Love with Poetry*. San Diego, NY, London: Harvest, 1999, p.311.

without having to know Latin. This presented a threat to the powers that be, and the church, for one, was highly displeased.

The Italian sonnet was developed by Dante and especially Petrarch and is therefore often called Petrarchan. It uses five rhymes and most often — in English — iambic pentameter. In the first eight lines the rhyme scheme is *abbaabba*; in the last six, it is some variation of *cdecde*. Thomas Wyatt introduced the sonnet to England and the Earl of Surrey modified the rhyme scheme, increasing the number of rhyming words from five to seven to better suit the English language which, compared to Italian, offers fewer rhyme possibilities. The English (or Shakespearean) sonnet is usually written in iambic pentameter. It has three four-line stanzas rhyming *abab cdcd efef* and a concluding rhymed couplet *gg*. Generally, the first twelve lines present a situation while the couplet comments and offers a summation. Poets can use the quatrains to explore their theme from three different perspectives, leading up to the ringing conclusion of the couplet.

By the late sixteenth century, most poets in Europe were writing sonnets; as Marilyn Hacker says in *An Exaltation of Forms*, "they were the rap music of the day," and poets have never stopped exploring their potential.

As befits a radical form, the sonnet has dozens, if not hundreds, of significant variations, and Canadians have played a part in this rich tradition, often blending the sonnet with other poetic forms. W. H. New's "Acoustics" uses seven rhymed couplets that echo each other both in sound and content ("Listen: when the summer sun began / *Lesson one: December will begin*."). Diana Brebner's "The Golden Lotus" is an English sonnet presented or (as Stephanie Bolster suggests in *Arc*: 51) "disguised" as couplets. George McWhirter writes slender sonnets, deliberately working with shorter lines, varied patterns of near rhyme and a rhythm that "runs perpendicular with the syntax; i.e., if there is metre, it doesn't just apply to the line by itself, but to the phrase flowing down the page."[20] Paul Dutton's "so'net 3" is also a lipogram, a poem that deliberately limits the letters it uses — in this case, to only the letters in the word "sonnet." Seymour Mayne draws on the haiku tradition to leave the small thumbprint of a word sonnet

---

20   George McWhirter, in correspondence with the editors, July 2004.

that imposes great weight on each short (in this case, one word) line ("Hail / peppered / the / air"). Mayne describes it as a "miniature" version of the sonnet, "concise and usually visual in effect."[21]

John Reibetanz' "Head and Torso of the Minotaur" is a paired sonnet written in blank verse (i.e., unrhymed iambic pentameter) that opens and closes with the same line, and Herménégilde Chiasson's bilingual "Apollo at Aberdeen" is an Italian sonnet written in lines with six strong accents in each, the traditional metre of the French sonnet.

THE TRADITIONAL FORM:

Italian (Petrarchan):

STANZAS:	Two stanzas, an octave and a sestet
METRE:	Iambic pentameter
RHYME:	*abbaabba cdecde* (the *cdecde* pattern often varies)
REPETITION:	None required
DISTINGUISHING FEATURE:	A turn or resolution (*volta*), often marked by a blank space, separates the octave and the sestet

English (Shakespearian):

STANZA:	Three quatrains and a concluding couplet
METRE:	Iambic pentameter
RHYME:	*abab cdcd efef gg*
REPETITION:	None required
DISTINGUISHING FEATURE:	Ends with a closing (often epigrammatic) couplet

---

21 Seymour Mayne, in correspondence with the editors, October 2003.

Archibald Lampman
(1861–1899)

THE KING'S SABBATH

Once idly in his hall King Olave sat
Pondering, and with his dagger whittled chips;
And one drew near to him with austere lips,
Saying, "To-morrow is Monday," and at that
The king said nothing, but held forth his flat
Broad palm, and bending on his mighty hips,
Took up and mutely laid thereon the slips
Of scattered wood, as on a hearth, and gat
From off the embers near, a burning brand.
Kindling the pile with this, the dreaming Dane
Sat silent with his eyes set and his bland
Proud mouth, tight-woven, smiling, drawn with pain,
Watching the fierce fire flare, and wax, and wane,
Hiss and burn down upon his shrivelled hand.

Kenneth Leslie
(1892–1974)

SONNET

The silver herring throbbed thick in my seine,
silver of life, life's silver sheen of glory;
my hands, cut with the cold, hurt with the pain
of hauling the net, pulled the heavy dory,
heavy with life, low in the water, deep
plunged to the gunwale's lips in the stress of rowing,
the pulse of rowing that puts the world to sleep,
world within world endlessly ebbing, flowing.
At length you stood on the landing and you cried,
with quick low cries you timed me stroke on stroke
as I steadily won my way with the fulling tide
and crossed the threshold where the last wave broke
and coasted over the step of water and threw
straight through the air my mooring line to you.

George Johnston
(1913–2004)

CATHLEEN SWEEPING

The wind blows, and with a little broom
She sweeps against the cold clumsy sky.
She's three years old. What an enormous room
The world is that she sweeps, making fly
A little busy dust! And here am I
Watching her through the window in the gloom
Of this disconsolate spring morning, my
Thoughts as small and busy as her broom.

Do I believe in her? I cannot quite.
Beauty is more than my belief will bear.
I've had to borrow what I think is true:
Nothing stays put until I think it through.
Yet, watching her with her broom in the dark air
I give it up. Why should I doubt delight?

———————

Margaret Avison
(b. 1918)

TENNIS

Service is joy, to see or swing. Allow
All tumult to subside. Then tensest winds
Buffet, brace, viol and sweeping bow.
Courts are for love and volley. No one minds
The cruel ellipse of service and return,
Dancing white galliardes at tape or net
Till point, on the wire's tip, or the long burn-
ing arc to nethercourt marks game and set.
Purpose apart, perched like an umpire, dozes,
Dreams golden balls whirring through indigo.
Clay blurs the whitewash but day still encloses
The albinos, bonded in their flick and flow.
Playing in musicked gravity, the pair
Score liquid Euclids in foolscaps of air

W. H. New
(b. 1938)

ACOUSTICS

Listen: when the summer sun began
       Lesson one: December will begin.
warming earth and air and every bud,
       worms will eat, and errant winds forbid
all creation dressed in sudden wonder;
       eloquence. Predestined sullen winter;
high up in the cherry orchards, white
       who appreciates its icy white
blossom sets, day approaches noon,
       blast, its adze-grey reaches? No-one.
crickets leap, chirp, chatter, and repeat:
       Cracked lips, sharp shattering retreat.
listen to the summer take its easing.
       Lesson two: remember echo's season.

———————

George McWhirter
(b. 1939)

AN ERA OF EASY MEAT AT LOCARNO

Where I ramble
by Jericho in the March
Mist and murk to take stock,
I glimpse an eagle perched
On a hemlock,
Above a bramble
Patch and rabbit that cannot dissemble
Its giddy nibbles in the grass, a pet bunny
Its bum left to bob like a yoo-hoo to a tummy
In a tree. Fast food, it will tremble
And jerk, then clog the eagle's throat,
Without redress, like a fur
Coat
On a hamburger.

—————

Paul Dutton

(b. 1943)

SO'NET 3

Onset tense: no tone to set,
no sense to note-not one; no, none.
So one soon tosses on to net
tenses, notes, tones. One soon sees one
to ten senses. Soon one's not too tense:
One's not sent to see eons nest
on stone tenets set to sonnet's sense.
One senses sonnets not sent to test,
sees no noose set, no nonsense, no
set one-ness. One senses entente, not
tense tones no sonnet's set to tote. So
tense not, testes, on notes to one's tot.
    Noon noses onto settee son's set on,
    one not seen to toss stone sonnet net on.

———————

Seymour Mayne
(b. 1944)

from WORD SONNETS

Hail

Hail
peppered
the
air
like
seed
as
you
were
lowered
below
the
frost
line.

John Reibetanz
(b. 1944)

HEAD AND TORSO OF THE MINOTAUR

1. Theseus at the Heart of the Labyrinth

The monster and the sacrifice are one,
the weapon anchored in the skull that bred it.
The first secret the hero has unearthed
disturbs him least — the torso of a woman
charging under the maned, snorting head.
His eye reads all as bestial, takes for proof
ripe breasts made monstrous by the drying blood.
The second will drive dream to sacrifice;
yet, only when their ship ties up at Naxos
does he take in what flickered by too quickly
as he plunged the horn into the skull's fountain.
Beyond the end of Ariadne's silk,
the snout's black nostrils, the jowl's slobbered fur:
eyes — human, hers, and anchored in them, his.

2. *Ukrainian Miner Rescued from Underground Explosion*

Only the eyes say human, the trunk and arms
speechless with animality, immured
in their caked hide, the head a clay melon
sprouting furry leafage. The eyes' thick lids
speak a familiar language of exhaustion;
and we can read the panic flaring from
the bloodshot whites, their anguish at the snarl
that has escaped from the ranged teeth where lips
once smiled, because our greed created this
slide into bestiality. Our will
to power carved his subterranean lair
and drove him down the scale of evolution
into a rubble-filled labyrinth where
the monster and the sacrifice are one.

———————————

Herménégilde Chiasson
(b. 1946)

APOLLO AT ABERDEEN
(translated by Jo-Anne Elder & Fred Cogswell)

quelqu'un m'a dit que tu n'écris plus qu'en anglais
I wonder if you do write about the same things
using new words to say the same old and sad meanings
les mots on pris d'autres tournures qu'en français

je suis trop lin sans doute pour me défaire l'oreille
credit cards sing they come and go but you will scream
in your own way even if their music fills your dream
j'entends ta voix intraduisible demain la veille

je me revois le jour où j'ai appris à lire
la lumière défonçait l'espace de ma prison
how far we came along yet I can hardly hear

prison is the same word in both languages you say
je sais mais maintenant je parle de la maison
de quoi parlerons-nous quand vous me visiterez

Kate Braid
(b. 1947)

from GLENN GOULD POEMS

6. Glenn Gould's Hands: A Sonnet

If I pull off these woollen mitts of mine
or shake your hand, who knows what harm may follow;
my fingers, knuckles, wrists — the lot — confined,
compressed or chilled, doomed to be impossible and slow.
Disaster of the fiercest kind if these,
these slender bridges of flesh and bone, these paths
for me to Bach, Beethoven, Bruckner, Strauss
and all the rest should suddenly collapse.

It's all a piece. The clothes, the hands, the quiet,
my need to live alone, by night. I do
not weed or dig. No crushing tools. I've quit
all cooking, seek out greasy spoons, to go
where no one knows me, wants to be my fan,
where no one knows me, wants to crush my hands.

———————

Diana Brebner

(1956–2001)

from THE GOLDEN LOTUS

"The pears fatten like little buddhas."
— Sylvia Plath, *The Manor Garden*

1. The Golden Lotus

We are always surprised that pears survive
so far north. Driving north, we watch the day

shrink in trees. It's behind us. We arrive.
Will it always be difficult to say:

I love you: caught at the cabin door, latch
unhooked? Yes, there are pears on the tree. And

a dead mouse in the sink. Bright fish to catch,
like kisses, in a lonely heaven. Hand

in hand. First things first. We go down the grass
stairway to the water. This is the blue

I would die for, the colour of tenderness,
and your forgiveness. Fish jump: silver, new.

In blue lakes, the golden lotus appears.
We sink our teeth into the yellow pears.

Anne Simpson
(b. 1956)

WAKING

The elm lies prone, its branches cut away:
soon chain saws will begin. I've woken far
from you. And you from me. Each day,
with coffee poured in cups, we leave ajar
the door that opens on a ragged lawn,
ghost irises and yellow daisies bent
and drifting from each other with a yawn,
as memory lifts and falls. Perhaps we meant
to conjure things so neither one could fail
or change. I see you standing in a blaze
of sun, the distant hills a kind of braille
we read in blue. I thought I'd kept each phrase.
But no, let's not give in to that disease
that slowly spreads until it takes down trees.

———————

Barbara Nickel
(b. 1966)

FOR PETER, MY COUSIN

The night you died I heard your cello shift —
a scraping in its corner of the barn.
Alfalfa pillowed it. White breath of pigs
was wreathed around the scroll; the cattle mourned.
For years its neck had rested by your ear.
Your bow across its strings and belly filled
the burlap sacks with apples, dusky tarns
of sound. You listened to that voice until
your marriage. Then she didn't let you play.
Her own voice, hoarse from children, saw you lean
in longing to the shovel, hurl the hay.
She felt your fingers press the strings in dream.
Your heart collapsed too soon — you died asleep.
Beside you she heard wood and horsehair weep.

———————

Shane Neilson
(b. 1975)

RURAL GOTHIC

And love as blight or the kind of drought
that kills all green, leaving no work
but to weep and level the scorched stalks
with mortgaged machinery; the weather-beaten
crops that couldn't stand pestilence, frost,
or love turned on itself. As soil erodes
and fronds arrest their growth, the season's lost
and fault is no one's. What's left are debts
that must be borne for another year. I've tried
to touch that man who'd throttle a neck
as he did a cracked drive shaft, his grip belied
by how much he felt each failure, a black
and hardened ruin. Love as negative, in reverse,
but still in terms of violence: a kind of verse.

STANZA

Stanzas, as can be seen in other chapters, are an important organizing principle for most fixed forms, but they also constitute intriguing forms in and of themselves. Stanzaic poems are divided into groups of metered and end-rhymed lines, and usually each group has the same number of lines. Beyond this, however, there are myriad patterns to choose from — and invent.

The word stanza means *room* or *apartment* in Italian. Much as you move from room to room in your own home, you move through a stanzaic poem — racing up the stairs or sauntering along the hallway; opening or closing doors; stopping suddenly, caught short by something previously unnoticed; or turning back, the familiar reminding you, perhaps, of something you meant to do. The pace, music and emotion of the tour depend upon how the poet selects and employs a stanza's central elements (rhyme and metre, phrase and sentence, line and stanza break, refrain and repetition) to develop and enhance meaning.

Over the centuries, various stanzas have been named, often to acknowledge an important poem, a popular pattern, or a particularly skilled poet. Eric Duncan's Spenserian stanza, "Drought," is one of the more common forms. Named after Edmund Spenser, who developed the pattern for "The Faerie Queene," the form consists of nine lines rhyming *ababbcbcc*. The first eight lines are in iambic pentameter and the ninth, with two more syllables, is an alexandrine (an iambic hexameter line, as in Duncan's: "For I | have <u>none</u> | to <u>spare</u> | — I <u>think</u> | of <u>months</u>| to <u>come</u>"). This is widely considered one of the most challenging, yet versatile of the stanza forms. For instance, the rhyme scheme offers various options for organizing content, of which *abab* | *bcbc* | *c* or *aba* | *bb* | *cbc* | *c* are just two possibilities.

Archibald Lampman's "The City of the End of Things" and Marjorie Pickthall's "Ebb Tide" show how seemingly small differences in metre and rhythm can work with content to create poems that sound and feel entirely different. Both poets use an *abab* rhyme scheme. Lampman's metre, however, rarely veers from a constant iambic tetrameter ("Of <u>mid</u> | night <u>streams</u> | un<u>known</u> | to <u>us</u>") while Pickthall's lines of primarily four, three, four and two strong accents rely on the frequent combination of two- and three-syllable feet, as in "And <u>hark</u> | for the <u>surge</u> | and the <u>strong</u> | <u>thun</u>der" and "<u>Here</u> he may | <u>lie</u> at | <u>ease</u> and | <u>won</u>der." And while Lampman's long stanzas are organized according to major shifts in narrative content, Pickthall's are all quatrains based on the metre and rhyme pattern. The overall effect, in Pickthall's poem, is a softer, slower pace and a deeply elegiac tone; in Lampman's, it's a relentless urgency that emphasizes the dystopian vision.

Poets often experiment with rhyme and metre to invent a pattern for one particular poem. This one-off pattern is called a nonce stanza. For example, Adam Sol in "The Conductor" has created a nonce form in which each stanza has seven loosely metered lines of four strong accents and an eighth line with two strong accents; the rhyme scheme, a subtle *abacdbdc*, often relies on assonance and consonance. This almost invisible pattern blends beautifully with what Sol is saying about how, against all odds, musicians obey the conductor and "… become / an orchestra in his sculpting hands."

THE TRADITIONAL FORM:

STANZAS: Usually four to nine lines: quatrains (4 lines), quintets (5 lines), sestets (6 lines), septets (7 lines), octets (8 lines) and Spenserian (9 lines); couplets and tercets are normally considered separate forms — see Couplet and Tercet chapters

METRE: Lines are metered

RHYME: Lines are end-rhymed

REPETITION: None required

NAMED PATTERNS: Among the poems in this chapter, four are examples of stanza patterns that have acquired their own names over the years. There are numerous others, which are described in most handbooks, including the resources listed in the bibliography at the end of this book. The patterns included in this chapter are:

- Long metre: tetrameter quatrains rhyming *abab* or *aabb* (Lampman's "The City of the End of Things," though his stanzas are organized in multiples of four — 8, 20, 16 etc.)
- Spanish quintilla: five lines of eight syllables each, or in iambic tetrameter rhyming *ababb* may also rhyme *ababa*, *abbab*, *abaab*, *aabab*, or *aabba* (Bliss Carman's "Low Tide on Grand Pré").
- Shakespearean sestets: iambic pentameter sestets rhyming *ababcc* (Charles Bruce's "Eastern Shore")
- Spenserian stanzas: nine-line stanzas rhyming *ababbcbcc*, the first eight in iambic pentameter and the ninth an alexandrine (Eric Duncan's "Drought")

Eric Duncan
(1858–1944)

DROUGHT

August returns, but not with plenty crowned;
    Thin, dwarfed, and light of head is all the grain.
The meagre hay was, ere its blossom, browned;
    The root crops withered, all for want of rain.
The cows for aftergrass do seek in vain,
    And through the boundless woods afar they roam.
They anger me; but when driven home again
    Their sad eyes plead for hay, and I am dumb,
For I have none to spare — I think of months to come.

Bliss Carman
(1861–1929)

VAGABOND SONG

There is something in the autumn that is native to my blood —
Touch of manner, hint of mood;
And my heart is like a rhyme,
With the yellow and the purple and the crimson keeping time.

The scarlet of the maples can shake me like a cry
Of bugles going by.
And my lonely spirit thrills
To see the frosty asters like a smoke upon the hills.

There is something in October sets the gypsy blood astir;
We must rise and follow her,
When from every hill of flame
She calls and calls each vagabond by name.

Bliss Carman
(1861–1929)

LOW TIDE ON GRAND PRÉ

The sun goes down, and over all
These barren reaches by the tide
Such unelusive glories fall,
I almost dream they yet will bide
Until the coming of the tide.

And yet I know that not for us,
By an ecstasy of dream
He lingers to keep luminous
A little while the grievous stream,
Which frets, uncomforted of dream —

A grievous stream, that to and fro
Athrough the fields of Acadie
Goes wandering, as if to know
Why one beloved face should be
So long from home and Acadie.

Was it a year or lives ago
We took the grasses in our hands,
And caught the summer flying low
Over the waving meadow lands,
And held it there between our hands?

The while the river at our feet —
A drowsy inland meadow stream —
At set of sun the after-heat
Made running gold, and in the gleam
We freed our birch upon the stream.

There down along the elms at dusk
We lifted dripping blade to drift,
Through twilight scented fine like musk,
Where night and gloom awhile uplift,
Nor sunder soul and soul adrift.

And that we took into our hands
Spirit of life or subtler thing —
Breathed on us there, and loosed the bands
Of death, and taught us, whispering,
The secret of some wonder-thing.

Then all your face grew light, and seemed
To hold the shadow of the sun;
The evening faltered, and I deemed
That time was ripe, and years had done
Their wheeling underneath the sun.

So all desire and all regret,
And fear and memory, were naught;
One to remember or forget
The keen delight our hands had caught;
Morrow and yesterday were naught.

The night has fallen, and the tide ...
Now and again comes drifting home,
Across these aching barrens wide,
A sigh like driven wind or foam:
In grief the flood is bursting home.

———————

Archibald Lampman
(1861–1899)

THE CITY OF THE END OF THINGS

Beside the pounding cataracts
Of midnight streams unknown to us
'Tis builded in the leafless tracts
And valleys huge of Tartarus.
Lurid and lofty and vast it seems;
It hath no rounded name that rings,
But I have heard it called in dreams
The City of the End of Things.

Its roofs and iron towers have grown
None knoweth how high within the night,
But in its murky streets far down
A flaming terrible and bright
Shakes all the stalking shadows there,
Across the walls, across the floors,
And shifts upon the upper air
From out a thousand furnace doors;
And all the while an awful sound
Keeps roaring on continually,
And crashes in the ceaseless round

Of a gigantic harmony.
Through its grim depths re-echoing
And all its wearing height of walls,
With measured roar and iron ring,
The inhuman music lifts and falls.
Where no thing rests and no man is,
And only fire and night hold sway;
The beat, the thunder and the hiss
Cease not, and change not, night nor day.

And moving at unheard commands,
The abysses and vast fires between,
Flit figures that with clanking hands
Obey a hideous routine;
They are not flesh, they are not bone,
They see not with the human eye,
And from their iron lips is blown
A dreadful and monotonous cry;
And whoso of our mortal race
Should find that city unaware,
Lean Death would smite him face to face,
And blanch him with its venomed air:
Or caught by the terrific spell,
Each thread of memory snapt and cut,
His soul would shrivel and its shell
Go rattling like an empty nut.

It was not always so, but once,
In days that no man thinks upon,
Fair voices echoed from its stones,
The light above it leaped and shone:
Once there were multitudes of men,
That built that city in their pride,
Until its might was made, and then
They withered age by age and died.
But now of that prodigious race,

Three only in an iron tower,
Set like carved idols face to face,
Remain the masters of its power;
And at the city gate a fourth,
Gigantic and with dreadful eyes,
Sits looking toward the lightless north,
Beyond the reach of memories;
Fast rooted to the lurid floor,
A bulk that never moves a jot,
In his pale body dwells no more,
Or mind, or soul, — an idiot!

But sometime in the end those three
Shall perish and their hands be still,
And with the master's touch shall flee
Their incommunicable skill.
A stillness absolute as death
Along the slacking wheels shall lie,
And, flagging at a single breath,
The fires shall moulder out and die.
The roar shall vanish at its height,
And over that tremendous town
The silence of eternal night
Shall gather close and settle down.
All its grim grandeur, tower and hall,
Shall be abandoned utterly,
And into rust and dust shall fall
From century to century;
Nor ever living thing shall grow,
Or trunk of tree, or blade of grass;
No drop shall fall, no wind shall blow,
Nor sound of any foot shall pass:
Alone of its accursèd state,
One thing the hand of Time shall spare,
For the grim Idiot at the gate
Is deathless and eternal there.

Pauline Johnson

(1862–1913)

THE TRAIN DOGS

Out of the night and the north;
  Savage of breed and of bone,
Shaggy and swift comes the yelping band,
Freighters of fur from the voiceless land
  That sleeps in the Arctic zone.

Laden with skins from the north,
  Beaver and bear and raccoon,
Marten and mink from the polar belts,
Otter and ermine and sable pelts —
  The spoils of the hunter's moon.

Out of the night and the north,
  Sinewy, fearless and fleet,
Urging the pack through the pathless snow,
The Indian driver, calling low,
  Follows with moccasined feet.

Ships of the night and the north,
  Freighters on prairies and plains,
Carrying cargoes from field and flood
They scent the trail through their wild red blood;
  The wolfish blood in their veins.

———————

Marjorie Pickthall

(1883–1922)

EBB TIDE

The Sailor's Grave at Clo-oose, V.I.

Out of the winds' and the waves' riot,
Out of the loud foam,
He has put in to a great quiet
And a still home.

Here he may lie at ease and wonder
Why the old ship waits,
And hark for the surge and the strong thunder
Of the full Straits,

And look for the fishing fleet at morning,
Shadows like lost souls,
Slide through the fog where the seal's warning
Betrays the shoals,

And watch for the deep-sea liner climbing
Out of the bright West,
With a salmon-sky and her wake shining
Like a tern's breast, —

And never know he is done for ever
With the old sea's pride,
Borne from the fight and the full endeavour
On an ebb tide.

Earle Birney
(1904–1995)

FROM THE HAZEL BOUGH

I met a lady
   on a lazy street
hazel eyes
   and little plush feet

her legs swam by
   like lovely trout
eyes were trees
   where boys leant out
hands in the dark and
   a river side
round breasts rising
   with the finger's tide

she was plump as a finch
   and live as a salmon
gay as silk and
   proud as a Brahmin

we winked when we met
   and laughed when we parted
never took time
   to be brokenhearted

but no man sees
   where the trout lie now
or what leans out
   from the hazel bough

Charles Bruce
(1906–1968)

EASTERN SHORE

He stands and walks as if his knees were tensed
To a pitching dory. When he looks far off
You think of trawl-kegs rolling in the trough
Of swaying waves. He wears a cap against
The sun on water, but his face is brown
As an old mainsail, from the eyebrows down.

He has grown old as something used and known
Grows old with custom; each small fading scar
Engrained by use and wear in plank and spar,
In weathered wood and iron, and flesh and bone.
But youth lurks in the squinting eyes, and in
The laughter wrinkles in the tanbark skin.

You know his story when you see him climb
The lookout hill. You know that age can be
A hill for looking; and the swaying sea
A lifetime marching with the waves of time.
Listen — the ceaseless cadence, deep and slow.
Tomorrow. Now. And years and years ago.

A. M. Klein

(1909–1972)

THE STILL SMALL VOICE

The candles splutter; and the kettle hums;
The heirloomed clock enumerates the tribes,
Upon the wine-stained table-cloth lie crumbs
Of matzoh whose wide scattering describes
Jews driven in far lands upon this earth.

The kettle hums; the candles splutter; and
Winds whispering from shutters tell re-birth
Of beauty rising in an eastern land,
Of paschal sheep driven in cloudy droves;
Of almond-blossoms colouring the breeze;
Of vineyards upon verdant terraces;
Of golden globes in orient orange-groves.
And those assembled at the table dream
Of small schemes that an April wind doth scheme,
And cry from out the sleep assailing them:
Jerusalem, next year! Next year, Jerusalem!

———————

P. K. Page
(b. 1916)

WATER AND MARBLE

And shall I tell him that the thought of him
turns me to water
and when his name is spoken pale still sky
trembles and breaks and moves like blowing water
that winter thaws its frozen drifts in water
all matter blurs, unsteady, seen through water
and I, in him, dislimn, water in water?

As true: the thought of him
has made me marble
and when his name is spoken blowing sky
settles and freezes in a dome of marble
and winter scals its floury drifts in marble
all matter double-locks as dense as marble
and I, in other's eyes, am cut from marble.

———————

Miriam Waddington
(1917–2004)

OLD WOMEN OF TORONTO

All old women sometimes come to this:
they go to live away, they cross ravines,
mornings they ride the subway, later look below
to read the red of dogwood and the print of snow.
They tread upon the contours of each month
with delicate feet that hardly sense its shape,
explore the mouth of March and with a hiss,
they spit at myth and swallow counter-bliss.

Their brows beetle, their plush hats tremble
they specially deplore without preamble
the palomino carpets on the lawns
steamy with manure in frosty air;
against all evidence and witnesses they'll swear
they never argued once or schemed to take
the room in front with the old Morris chair,
and partial view, at least, of the bright lake.

Michael Crummey
(b. 1965)

THE NAKED MAN

Shower room's peace shattered by boys launched
like rockets, their racket sudden as rain
on a tin roof. Shyness sharp as a sprain
makes him wince at the sight of his paunch,

his penis crouched in its thicket of curls.
But the boys ignore the naked man beside
them, their voices pitched toward registers
beyond hearing, skin translucent white,

everything about them in ascendance,
inching toward their adult heights
without hesitation or reluctance.
They orbit his silence like satellites

trailing the dead weight of stars —
there's no way to warn them what lies ahead
and he's torn by a father's helpless regret,
seeing them so unguarded, so free of scars.

———————

Adam Sol
(b. 1969)

THE CONDUCTOR

With all the power rushing past,
amazing that he doesn't fall.
We stare at his galloping back,
his sharp gestures an angry teacher's.
No wonder we get a little nervous.
On the platform he seems small,
whipping his baton so it curves,
a peacock feather.

Arrayed against him, musicians in black
rub horsehair on catgut, burst their lungs
forcing air through tubes, or strike
surfaces of assorted tensions
with what can only be called relish.
I worry that if the man does one thing wrong —
instead of French horns, asks for English —
the whole fiction

will explode: mass fermata, winds
discarding chewed spit-swollen reeds,
oboes flung at violins
they've always resented, trombones at last
up front, carousing, brutally loud …
I almost want them to succeed,
but he restrains them, saves the crowd.
Brahams advances

in stately fashion, as he deserves.
And though there's plenty to see, for once
our eyes are not our first concern.
The players, tamed, grumble in pairs,
but obey the conductor's stern commands
like good grandchildren. They become
an orchestra in his sculpting hands.
They trill the air.

———

Zachariah Wells
(b. 1976)

FOOL'S ERRAND

My mother sent me into the swirling
Bowl of stirred-up curdled milk
Our valley was, wild with wind and skirling
Snow that fastened onto lashes, there to melt
And bead and break mute light, unfurling
Bows like multi-coloured scraps of silk.

Bring them in, she said, they'll freeze to death
Out there. Out there then I went,
Tripping through the hip-high snow, each breath
A wet-rag gasp, as weaving wind sent
Shuttling snow between my teeth and hooked a snowdrop wreath
Around my neck. When I found them, he was bent

Over her back, his forepaws clutched her rump.
I tried hard to pull him out of her,
But still he blindly pumped and pumped,
Eyes shut against the storm that heaped snow in his hair.
I hauled off and handed him one solid thump
Which only shook his haunches bare.

I stumbled home and left them there.

SYLLABICS

Since the sixteenth century, English has been primarily an accentual-syllabic language, that is, one in which each word is made up of a series of syllables that are each given more or less stress when spoken. By writing in metre, most poets mean they are measuring the number of syllables, as well as the pattern of strong and soft accents (or stresses) on those syllables when they're spoken aloud.

However, poets have always loved to experiment, and one of their pleasures has been to count only the number of syllables in a line, regardless of where the accents fall. This is called syllabics. It gained some popularity in the early twentieth century when, in England, Robert Bridges and his daughter Elizabeth Daryush developed the form and later, in the United States, Marianne Moore and others followed suit.

As Lewis Turco explains in *The New Book of Forms*, there are three main syllabic options:

- using the same number of syllables in every line,
- establishing a syllable pattern in stanza one (which may vary from line to line), and following it in each subsequent stanza, and
- varying the number of syllables per line within certain limits (e.g., each line has a minimum of seven and a maximum of nine syllables).

(How syllables are counted can vary, especially given regional inflections and differences in pronunciation. So you might count "buoy" as one syllable, or two.)

By organizing lines by syllable count regardless of where the accents fall, regularly metered patterns are de-emphasized. In fact, the syllabic writer will often pick an uneven number of syllables per line, to avoid falling into a regular pattern of soft / strong accents. This can be easy to do and a surprising number of casual sentences fall into the iambic pattern, e.g., I'd <u>like</u> | to <u>have</u> | a <u>bur</u>| ger <u>and</u> | some <u>fries</u>.

Syllable count creates a subtle form of poetry, sometimes more visual than aural in effect. It is the closest a poet can come to free verse yet still maintain a certain writing "discipline," and it works not only in very short poems such as Daniel David Moses' "The Hands," but can also be sustained throughout a longer poem, as in Russell Thornton's "The Cherry Laurel."

For another challenge, Phyllis Gotlieb and Richard Outram have chosen to combine a strict syllable count with a regular metre, thus giving their poems added intensity. The effect of this in Gotlieb's "Death's Head," with the addition of frequent end rhyme and the repeating phrases, "take in a breath," "give out a breath," produces a strong feeling of incantation. In "Round of Life," Outram balances a regular syllable count (8, 3, 8, 3) with regularly rhymed and accented lines (in addition to various internal rhymes) to create a poem that is irresistible — inescapable — in both sound and sense.

Although the traditional Japanese sound in forms such as the haiku is not strictly a syllable, it is often adapted to English as three lines of 5, 7 and 5 syllables. Some of the traditional Greek forms have also been adapted to English by substituting strong accents for long vowels and soft ones for short. The Sapphic stanza — named after the Greek poet Sappho who lived in the early seventh century BC — often becomes, in English, a four line stanza with 11, 11, 11 and 5 syllables, organized into a specific pattern of accents in each line. Barbara Myers adheres to this pattern in "Dream Prison." Her line "<u>Pow</u>er <u>fail</u>ure. <u>Wak</u>ing, you <u>try</u> the <u>switch</u>es" shows how the eleven-syllable line works. (An alternate pattern for the long line is to replace the second strong accent with a soft one.) And "<u>crum</u>pled-up <u>sleep</u>er" shows how the five-syllable line works. Jay Macpherson applies the syllable count but varies the traditional pattern of accents in the long lines in "Some Ghosts & Some Ghouls."

Another well-known syllabic pattern, probably of French medieval origin, is the five-line cinquain. American poet Adelaide Crapsey adapted it to English, giving it a pattern of 2, 4, 6, 8 and 2 syllables per line. Nancy Bennett's "The Ghost of His Hand" is a fine example of why the cinquain's intensity is often compared to the Japanese haiku.

THE TRADITIONAL FORM:

Syllabics

STANZAS:	An unlimited number of stanzas
METRE:	Replaced by syllable count, although poets may add a metric element as well; the pattern is up to the poet
RHYME:	None required
REPETITION:	None required

Sapphics

STANZAS:	An unlimited number of stanzas
METRE:	Replaced by a syllable count of 11, 11, 11, 5 in each stanza. The pattern in the 11-syllable lines is strong/soft/strong/soft (or strong)/strong/soft/soft/strong/soft/strong/soft; in the 5-syllable lines it's strong/soft/soft/strong/soft
RHYME:	None required
REPETITION:	None required

Cinquain

STANZAS:	One 5-line stanza
METRE:	Replaced by a syllable count of 2, 4, 6, 8, 2
RHYME:	None required
REPETITION:	None required

Phyllis Gotlieb
(b. 1926)

DEATH'S HEAD

at 3 a.m. I run my tongue
around my teeth (take in a breath)
(give out a breath) take one more step
approaching death. my teeth are firm
and hard and white (take in a breath)
incisors bite and molars grind
(give out a breath) the body lying
next to mine is sweet and warm
I've heard that worms (take in a breath)
don't really eat (give out a breath)
the coffin meat of human kind
and if they did I wouldn't mind
that's what I heard (take in a breath)
(and just in time) I think it's all
a pack of lies. I know my flesh
will end in slime. the streets are mean
and full of thieves. the children in
the sleeping rooms (give out a breath)
walk narrowly upon my heart
the animal beneath the cloth
submerged rises to any bait
of lust or fury, love or hate
(take in a breath) my orbic skull
is eminently frangible
so delicate a shell to keep
my brains from spillage. still my breath
goes in and out and nearer death

and yet I seem to get to sleep

Richard Outram

(1930–2005)

ROUND OF LIFE

Let us the fruit of Love's pursuit
discover;
Of Jenny Wren, of speckled hen,
of plover.

Here is an egg. Without a leg
to stand on:
When laid to rest, it must the nest
abandon.

Death is the norm: this perfect form
before us
We contemplate, may to our fate
restore us.

Herein is held, without a weld,
or caulking,
A germ of flight, '…world of delight,'
& squawking:

Which is, when broached, & sometimes poached,
devoured;
That thereby we may likewise be
empowered.

Jay Macpherson
(b. 1931)

from THE WAY DOWN

Some Ghosts & Some Ghouls

While we loved those who never read our poems,
Answered our letters, said the simple things we
Waited so long for, and were too polite to
    See we were crying,

Irony fed us: for the days we watched our
Chances to please them, nights in rumpled beds lay
Gored by their phantoms, guilty most of suffering,
    We were rewarded.

While we admired how ignorance became them,
Coldness adorned, they came at length to trust us,
Made us their mirrors: last their hopeless loves to
    Us they confided.

They were our teachers: what we are, they made us.
Cautious our converse, prudent our behaviour,
Guarded our faces: we behind them lurking,
    Greedy, devourers.

Barbara Myers

DREAM PRISON

Power failure. Waking, you try the switches,
push them. Nothing. Rooms remain dark, their edges
blurred and dreaming. You're the one dreaming. Wake now,
                        crumpled-up sleeper.

See your body curled on the bed, insensate,
morning's call a light-bringing far-off praying.
Sleep-imprisoned powerless mortal being,
                       why do you struggle?

Daniel David Moses
(b. 1952)

THE HANDS

Yes, our faces are ten blanks
but bearded with the ghosts of
quarter moons. So we are wise,
wiser than you who go clothed
in fur, than you who have eyes.

Russell Thornton
(b. 1959)

THE CHERRY LAUREL

The women who would gather in the vale
chewed cherry laurel leaves; when the poison
took hold and ushered them into frenzy,
they would see the vale was a hovering
of matter, a glittering haze; the earth
their bare feet danced on, and that had brought forth
everything around them, would — if they
threw off the names they had used for themselves —
begin to reveal to them what there was
of eternity in the world.
                    The vale
could open into a being, human,
yet other, whose name was a limitless,
pure embrace in an instant with no end;
then could close again and be a chaos
of innumerable identities
interspersed with abyss upon abyss.
It could pour blind currents of life, of death,
through the women's living skulls, and plunge them
into metamorphoses — so they might
suddenly know more than any mortal,
having become the vale itself, knowing.
Some would never return from such knowing,
and collapse and die. But others would now
be called Daphne, the name for the laurel,
and be priestesses.
                  The light of the vale
is in love with those frenzied ones — the rays
sent as from Apollo still following

the woman who ran from him and escaped
when she was changed into a tree; even
the fate of Apollo's love is held here
in the laurel branches. Here, your own fate,
though you do not know that fate, pours through you,
while the light, the vegetation, and rock,
so bright, so mysteriously exact,
are all a moving stillness, about to speak.

— Vale of Tempe/Larissa, Greece

Nancy Bennett
(b. 1962)

THE GHOST OF HIS HAND

>   Shallow
> Bruises blush   blue
>   Hidden by my sweet smile
>   Bruises fade but their ghosts always
>   Linger

TERCET

Tercets are three line verse units that either stand alone or make up part of a larger stanza. They are easily as versatile as couplets, perhaps more so because the third line gives added room to develop content and use rhyme and metre to advantage. In Ann Wilkinson's "Tigers Know From Birth," for instance, the third line is abbreviated to three strong accents, releasing the energy and emotion of the preceding longer lines with an oomph we feel bodily as we read.

There is some disagreement among experts on the difference between tercet and triplet, but often when the three lines rhyme *aaa* (as in the opening of "Tigers ...") they are called triplets. Enclosed tercets rhyme *aba*, as in most of Phyllis Webb's "The Second Hand." Throughout Webb's poem, the insistent recurrence of internal rhyme ("of the tick, the tock, the icy draught / of a clock's arms ...") and end rhyme ("not," "knot," "not," "caught") reinforces a sense of "the pressing stress of time."

This succinct form offers numerous other rhyme and metre combinations. Duncan Campbell Scott's regular tetrameter lines in "A Night in June" rhyme *abb*; enhancing the feeling of a seemingly endless, inescapable heat wave. At the other end of the spectrum, Marianne Bluger's lines of either two or three strong accents and a free-form rhyme scheme help convey the sense of aimless drifting in "In Oak."

Like couplets, tercets are not usually considered a stanza form in their own right, but they are integral to several other forms such as the haiku, and are a main feature of the villanelle and terzanelle.

Terza rima was invented by Dante as the engine that pulled his Divine Comedy into the depths of hell and up again toward heaven (with obvious reference to the Christian Trinity). Its series of linked envelope rhymes (*aba bcb cdc* etc.) create a pattern that steadily pulls the reader through the poem. The form usually ends with either a single line or a couplet, and in English, is usually written in iambic pentameter. Both Sharon Thesen's "The Broken

Cup" and Stephen Heighton's "Blackjack," however, rely primarily on the unifying effect of rhyme rather than metre. When written in fourteen lines, terza rima can be a variation of the sonnet (called, fittingly, the terza rima sonnet), rhyming *aba bcb cdc ded ee*.

THE TRADITIONAL FORM:

Tercet

STANZAS:	Three lines each; no set number (not usually considered a stanza form)
METRE:	Lines are usually metered (iambic pentameter) but no set pattern required
RHYME:	Lines are end-rhymed but no set pattern required
REPETITION:	None required

Terza rima

STANZAS:	Three lines each; no set number
METRE:	Lines are usually metered (iambic pentameter) but no set pattern required
RHYME:	*aba*, *bcb*, *cdc* etc.
REPETITION:	None required
DISTINGUISHING FEATURE:	Final stanza can be a single line or a couplet; in either case, the line(s) rhyme with the middle line of the preceding stanza

Duncan Campbell Scott
(1862–1947)

A NIGHT IN JUNE

The world is heated seven times,
  The sky is close above the lawn,
  An oven when the coals are drawn.

There is no stir of air at all,
  Only at times an inward breeze
  Turns back a pale leaf in the trees.

Here the syringa's rich perfume
  Covers the tulip's red retreat,
  A burning pool of scent and heat.

The pallid lightning wavers dim
  Between the trees, then deep and dense
  The darkness settles more intense.

A hawk lies panting in the grass,
  Or plunges upward through the air,
  The lightning shows him whirling there.

A bird calls madly from the eaves,
  Then stops, the silence all at once
  Disturbed, falls dead again and stuns.

A redder lightning flits about,
  But in the north a storm is rolled
  That splits the gloom with vivid gold;

Dead silence, then a little sound,
   The distance chokes the thunder down,
   It shudders faintly in the town.

A fountain plashing in the dark
   Keeps up a mimic dropping strain;
   Ah! God, if it were really rain!

Anne Wilkinson
(1910–1961)

TIGERS KNOW FROM BIRTH

My bones predict the striking hour of thunder
And water as I huddle under
       The tree the lightning renders

I'm hung with seaweed, winding in its caul
The nightmare of a carp whose blood runs cold,
       A crab who apes my crawl

My lens is grafted from a jungle eye
To focus on the substance of a shadow's
       Shadow on the sky

My forest filtered drum is pitched to hear
The serpent split the grass before the swish
       Is feather in my ear

I've learned from land and sea of every death
Save one, the easy rest, the little catnap
       Tigers know from birth

———————

Phyllis Webb
(b. 1927)

THE SECOND HAND

Here, Love, whether we love or not
involves the clock and its ignorant hands
tying our hearts in a lover's knot;

now, whether we flower or not
requires a reluctance in the hour;
yet we cannot move, in the present caught

in the embrace of to be or not;
dear, shall we move our hands together,
or must we bear the onslaught

of the tick, the tock, the icy draught
of a clock's arms swinging themselves together —
or now shall we kiss where once we laughed?

all time is sadness but the heart is not
unmoved in the minute of the dancing measure,
for if in the pressing stress of time

the dancer stays, or act is mime,
hands must break by being caught
as the clock covers its face with an evil weather.

————————————

Marianne Bluger
(b. 1945)

IN OAK

Where will you drift, Sadie,
now that you lie
in the velvet boat

with your shot-silk dress,
the jade at your throat
and those ferret eyes shut —

where will you float,
now you have had to let go —
you who would always row?

————————————

Sharon Thesen

(b. 1946)

THE BROKEN CUP

Bits of prosody fall near what remains of me
that drifts on the sofa in a trance
made of loves, lazy rivers, unmended crockery.

I feel so broken now by a too-long dance.
Shot exhausted horses fall behind the stadium
and shards of mirror lance

What could have been a fatal wound, fatal tedium
or a spiritual lesson to have learned
endlessly postponed like closure & delirium.

One wants clear endings, beginnings to burn
big holes through old obdurate patterns, one wants
love to "triumph" as it were but not to earn

A thousand bardos, a daily headache, an ounce
of comfrey for a cure when I am acting up
& slink around ashamed of getting trounced

At life & coping, nearly. Like certain music
refuses transcendence (that strange vulgarity),
and how I threw the broken cup

Away because I know to hope for clarity
where things are broken is just to lie.

Richard Sanger
(b. 1960)

3: WHO WAS THAT? I ASK …

Who was that? I ask. You've been gone for ages.
Like the phone you've just returned to its cradle,
I lie in bed alone. Everything changes.

Like the phone to its cradle, I return
Down the hallway, my lawful wedded one,
To wait, shivering, at the door for your word.

Don't enter yet. I asked a question.
Pomegranates. Persimmons. Papyrus.
Who is it? I am the Prince of Shades,

I answer to no one. Answer the question.
I have said who I am, and who I am
Are all the things I've said, words I've dressed in

And, shivering, undressed in, speeches I've addressed,
Dispatched, enraptured, to the airy blue,
All the robes I've worn, roles I've played for you,

I could be anyone, Coeur de Lion,
Or the Crookback come with halting step,
With gifts, persimmons, papyrus … I lie,

I'm not myself at all, I'm all mixed up,
Things I've read, I've said, I was, head over heels,
Above, below, intoxicated — No,

No, I'll drop this pretence, drop the subject,
Drop this cloak, my clothes, my sunglasses, my sword,
And find the door I'll come naked through
To meet (in the bath, in the bed) naked you.

Steven Heighton
(b. 1961)

BLACKJACK

Hit: to take another card, and risk breaking.
Stand: to stick with what you have.

The dealer is dailiness, and the asking —
hit or stand? — comes more often than you guess.
Missed cues can fill a life. Or you signal wrong,

the house responds, no recourse. Standing with less
may be safer — you know the odds — but even then
the temptation is to hit. Sometimes loss

at long odds looks better than a sure win;
as if winning were a sure thing, ever.
In some dreams a familiar house will open

into unsuspected rooms, door after door
glides ajar, yet you hang back and consciousness
cuts in like an eviction. But what if you were

not so anxious to wake back into your less
uncharted life, and chanced those farther rooms …?
Caution cancels love's richer part; eros,

sequestered in home safety, always seems
to die by inches. The house wins by turning
its people into furniture. Many tombs

are made of unplayed cards. It's me I'm warning
here. Hit when the asking happens. The house
may have its system, but you're not through learning.

TRIOLET

A French fixed form dating back to the 1300s, the triolet made a brief appearance in English in the sixteenth century, but didn't take hold until the late 1800s. As a short version of the rondel, it is technically a member of the rondeau family and features two refrains and two rhymes in just eight lines.

Because the two refrains take up five of the poem's eight lines, this form poses a particular challenge — how to avoid tedium. As noted in *The New Princeton Handbook of Poetic Terms*, the poet must manage "… the intricate repetition so that it seems natural and inevitable, … achieving, in the repetitions, variety of meaning or, at least, a shift in emphasis."

In English, the triolet is usually written as a single, self-contained stanza, but its brevity invites possibilities for a sequence, as in Christopher Wiseman's "Triolets for Ken." To avoid monotony, poets often dispense with the rhyme scheme, use free verse rather than metered lines, change internal punctuation to vary the meaning of a refrain line, and/or change words or phrases in the refrains.

Elise Partridge's "Vuillard Interior" is a good example of how altering the refrain can introduce variety ("Against brown walls, the servant bends / under the lamp, the servant bends / knotting, nodding, the servant blends"). Joy Kogawa's "Bread to Stone" is unrhymed and unmetered, but an even more notable variation is that line four is not a refrain at all. This adds to the poem's impact when the two opening lines reappear at the end. Sandy Shreve offers another variation to the refrain. In "Landing," she attaches each phrase in the first line to a different sentence each time the line reappears, to shift both its meaning and, by moving the pause (caesura), its rhythm. So, for example, in the first instance "What you see is what you get / to come home to. …" becomes, in the second instance, "… charms / what you see. Is what you'll get / drawn into …" In this way, the refrain is made to feel new each time we hear it.

THE TRADITIONAL FORM:

STANZAS: One octet

METRE: Lines are usually iambic trimeter or iambic tetrameter

RHYME: *ABaAabAB* (capitals indicate refrains)

REPETITION: The first refrain appears three times as lines 1, 4, 7; the second appears twice as lines 2 and 8

Joy Kogawa
(b. 1935)

BREAD TO STONE

turned to stone
she asked for bread
we offered cakes
and as she waited
the food
within her grasp
turned to stone
she asked for bread

Christopher Wiseman
(b. 1936)

TRIOLETS FOR KEN

> *The recollection of happiness is no longer happiness.*
> *The recollection of pain is still pain.*
>
> — from the film *The Secret of Nandy*

1.

Three times a year the nightmare comes again.
Time heals a lot but this appalls me yet —
The plunge off a cliff, terrified, alone.
Three times a year the nightmare comes again.
Down, down, grey sea, sharp rocks, but then no pain

As half way down I wake, caught in some net.
Three times a year this nightmare comes again.
Time heals, they say, but this appalls me yet.

2.

There is no happy music, Schubert said.
We were told before we sang — the cliff, the fall,
His body broken. The oldest of us dead.
There is no happy music, Schubert said,
Though we choirboys went into the church and tried.
Smashed on rocks. The violence filled us all.
There is no happy music, Schubert said.
We heard before we sang. The cliff. The fall.

3.

He collected seabirds' eggs and wanted more.
He little thought he'd wreck my dreams today
As he clambered Bempton cliffs, feeling so sure,
Collecting seabirds' eggs and wanting more.
Shrieking gulls, rocks falling, the sea's huge roar,
His screams — his last song — drowned in that *forte*.
He wanted seabirds' eggs, and wanted more,
And never thought he'd wreck my dreams today.

1945

Susan McCaslin
(b. 1947)

TRIOLET FOR THE AMPHETAMINE AFFLICTED

"Dear Dr. Hormone feed me for my dinner
those little pills so slippery and so cool;
just jazz me up; I want to be a winner.
Dear Dr. Hormone feed me for my dinner
those little pick-me-ups that make me thinner.
You know I used to think I was a fool
till Dr. Hormone fed me for my dinner
those little pills so slippery and so cool."

Sandy Shreve
(b. 1950)

LANDING

What you see is what you get
to come home to. Flickering in the night,
the city flirts with its own shadow, charms
what you see. Is what you'll get
drawn into the front porch lit with someone
waiting eagerly, or a darkened door?
What you see, is. What you get
to come home to flickers in the night.

Elise Partridge
(b. 1958)

VUILLARD INTERIOR

Against brown walls, the servant bends
over the coverlet she mends —
brown hair, brown flocking, a dun hand
under the lamp, the servant bends
over the coverlet she mends
draped across her broad brown skirts;
knotting, nodding, the servant blends
into the coverlet she mends.

———————

Danielle Janess
(b. 1978)

NIGHT, HORNBY ISLAND

In the breath of the tent
I held her small hand
while you and I made love. She stirred and sent,
in the breath of the tent
her fingers to search for my breast. Bent
toward you, laughing despite our plans,
in the breath of the tent,
I held her small hand.

VILLANELLE

The villanelle originated in Italy and appeared in France in the sixteenth century. What began as a loose form for pastoral themes requiring only the use of a refrain, gradually became a more structured form embracing a wide variety of subjects. By the seventeenth century the form had evolved into a poem that turned on two rhymes and two refrains in an unlimited number of tercets plus a closing quatrain.

The English version, which came into fashion in the nineteenth century, limited the villanelle to six stanzas. Lines 1 and 3 of the first tercet alternate as line 3 in the others, and together form the closing couplet in the quatrain. The form's challenge lies in creating an interesting poem that develops, rather than merely repeats, its content. Add to this the limited *ab* rhyme scheme over nineteen lines, and the poet also faces the difficulty of making the poem sing, rather than grate on the ear.

The villanelle's restrictions, like those of so many set forms, can become strengths. Eli Mandel, for instance, takes advantage of the incessant repetition to steadily deepen the sweetly mournful metaphor of the circling carousel in "City Park Merry-Go-Round." Bruce Meyer's "The Ferry to South Baymouth" shows how enjambment can both vary the emphasis of the repeated lines and help soften the recurring rhymes. ("… tiny stars / that define each wave …" "… her eye explores / and defines each wave …" "All that matters / as she defines each wave …"). And of course, the repeating lines also mirror the endless repetition (and peace) of the waves as they reflect his daughter's eyes — a hint of immortality, of life carrying on with his daughter.

As with the triolet, contemporary poets often vary or dispense with the villanelle's rhyme and metre to keep the form from calling too much attention to itself. They also often play with the repeated lines — as when Molly Peacock, in "Little Miracle," not only alters the refrain line, but adds to it the phrase "we're here," (from the non-refrain line in stanza one) to close the poem.

An American variation of the villanelle is the terzanelle (see David Waltner-Toews' "Woods"). Lines 1 and 3 of the terzanelle's first stanza are repeated only once, either as lines 2 and 4 or 3 and 4 of the final quatrain. The second line of each tercet becomes the third line of the next one, all the way through to the quatrain, creating a terza rima rhyme scheme (i.e., *aba*, *bcb*, *cdc*, etc.).

THE TRADITIONAL FORM:

Villanelle

STANZAS: Six stanzas; the first five are tercets and the sixth is a quatrain

METRE: Usually all lines have a common meter or syllable count (the pattern is up to the poet)

RHYME: $A^1bA^2 / abA^1 / abA^2 / abA^1 / abA^2 / abA^1A^2$ (capitals indicate refrains; the numbered letters, i.e., $A^1 \& A^2$, represent rhymed, but otherwise different lines)

REPETITION: As shown in the rhyme scheme, lines 1 and 3 of the opening tercet alternate as line 3 of the subsequent tercets and together provide lines 3 and 4 of the quatrain

Terzanelle

STANZAS: Six stanzas; the first five are tercets and the sixth is a quatrain

METRE: Usually all lines have a common meter or syllable count (the pattern is up to the poet)

RHYME: $A^1BA^2 / bCB / cDC / dED / eFE / fA^1FA^2$ (or $fF\ A^1A^2$) (capitals indicate refrains; the numbered letters, i.e., $A^1 \& A^2$, represent rhymed, but otherwise different lines)

REPETITION: As shown in the rhyme scheme, lines 1 and 3 of the opening tercet are repeated as lines 2 and 4 (or 3 and 4) of the final quatrain; line 2 of each tercet is repeated once, as line 3 of the following tercet (line 2 of the last tercet may be repeated as either line 3 or 2 of the quatrain)

Susie Frances Harrison

(ALIAS SERANUS)

(1859-1935)

CATHARINE PLOUFFE

This grey-haired spinster, Catharine Plouffe —
    Observe her, a contrast to convent chits,
At her spinning wheel, in the room in the roof.

Yet there are those who believe that the hoof
    Of a horse is nightly heard as she knits —
This grey-haired spinster, Catharine Plouffe —

Stockings of fabulous warp and woof,
    And that old Benedict's black pipe she permits
At her spinning wheel, in the room in the roof,

For thirty years. So the gossip. A proof
    Of her constant heart? Nay. No one twits
This grey-haired spinster, Catharine Plouffe;

The neighbours respect her, but hold aloof,
    Admiring her back as she steadily sits
At her spinning wheel, in her room in the roof.

Will they ever marry? Just ask her. Pouf!
    She would like you to know she's not lost her wits —
This grey-haired spinster, Catharine Plouffe,
At her spinning wheel, in her room in the roof.

———————

P. K. Page
(b. 1916)

THE CASTLE

It is the stress that holds the structure up.
Birds in its turrets tilt it not at all.
Balance is inner, centred in the keep.

Marble and timber crumble as we sleep.
Centuries of creeper cannot sustain a wall.
It is the stress that holds the structure up.

Lovers in spirals, turning in the deep
well of their rapture, dizzyingly recall
balance is inner, centred in the keep.

Patients, post-crisis, feel the fever drop.
The pendulum begins its swing from ill to well.
It is the stress that holds the structure up.

Whoever — dreaming — dances a tightrope
knows where is balance, just before the fall!
Balance is inner, centred in the keep.

Insomnia, pain and trouble have a stop
definitive, sudden, at the terminal.
It was the stress that held the structure up.
But balance is inner, centred in the keep.

Eli Mandel

(1922-1992)

CITY PARK MERRY-GO-ROUND

Freedom is seldom what you now believe.
Mostly you circle round and round the park:
Night follows day, these horses never leave.

Like children, love whatever you conceive,
See then your world as lights whirled in the dark.
Freedom is seldom what you now believe.

Your world moves up and down or seems to weave
And still you pass you pass the same ringed mark.
Night follows day, these horses never leave.

You thought your past was here, you might retrieve
That wild illusion whirling in the dark.
Freedom is seldom what you now believe.

Sick on that circle you begin to grieve.
You wish the ride would end you could escape the park.
Night follows day, these horses never leave.

Mostly you circle round and round the park.
You'd give your life now to be free to leave.
Freedom is seldom what you now believe.
Night follows day, these horses never leave.

———————

Molly Peacock
(b. 1947)

LITTLE MIRACLE

No use getting hysterical.
The important part is: we're here.
Our lives are a little miracle.

My hummingbird-hearted schedule
beats its shiny frenzy, day into year.
No use getting hysterical —

it's always like that. The oracle
a human voice could be is shrunk by fear.
Our lives are a little miracle

— we must remind ourselves — whimsical,
and lyrical, large and slow and clear.
(No use getting hysterical!)

All words other than *I love you* are clerical,
dispensable, and replaceable, my dear,
Our inner lives are a miracle.

They beat their essence in the coracle
our ribs provide, the watertight boat we steer
through others' acid, hysterical
demands. Ours is the miracle: *we're here*.

David Waltner-Toews
(b. 1948)

from COMING UP FOR AIR

Woods

I do not know whose woods those are. I do not care
to know. We fly above them, see the fox along the trees escape
into the shadows, pausing. We glide along the river's graceful turn

of phrase among the stuttering urban landscapes,
above the maples, poplars, oak, the green-roofed barns.
To know we fly above them, see the fox along the trees, escape

into clouds: enough. Let them stand arms akimbo, wish us good, or harm.
We are above all that — the truckers and the market — our heads
above the maples, poplars, oak, the green-roofed barns,

where farmers walk from shadows, smooth sun-warmed wood,
hitch Clydesdales to the plough. It is illusory to think
we are above all that — the truckers and the market — that heads

can somehow dis-attach from stomachs, that without bread and drink
there can be dreams. My hopes for earth's redemption yawn,
hitch Clydesdales to the plough. It is illusory to think

it matters more who owns the woods than that the woods are
there. I do not know whose woods those are. I do not care.
There can be dreams. My hopes for earth's redemption yawn
into the shadows, pausing. We glide along the river's graceful turn.

Carole Glasser Langille

CROWS

What shall we do with a murder of crows
in Kentville? Thousands of birds.
When they light they're as dark as their shadows.

Should we string them broken-necked from trees? Blow
off their heads? Something's undone in the breeze.
What shall we do with the murder of crows?

Loud speakers sound cries from their foes
but it just makes crows nervous.
When they light they're as dark as their shadows.

Gardens bleed light in the sun's orange glow.
Apples line bins. Pine sharpens the air.
What shall we do with a murder of crows?

Both sides are his dark side. The blackest crow
throws his lot in with the rest: good luck, bad luck.
When they light they're as dark as their shadows.

These omens mock us; there's nowhere to go
in Kentville. If one crow's sorrow, what are a thousand?
What shall we do with a murder of crows?
When they light they're as dark as their shadows.

Bruce Meyer
(b. 1957)

THE FERRY TO SOUTH BAYMOUTH

My daughter's eyes are blue as Georgian Bay
and sparkle with the glint of tiny stars
that define each wave on a summer's day;

for among the vacationers who have run away
with all their necessities packed in cars,
my daughter's eyes are blue as Georgian Bay.

This is her first summer. She has a way
of measuring things as her eye explores
and defines each wave on a summer's day

with the luxury of unencumbered sight. I say
boat but all she sees are endless waters —
my daughter's eyes are blue as Georgian Bay.

Her little hand points to a gull, the sway
and lilt of its wings on wind. All that matters
as she defines each wave on a summer's day

and sparkles with the glint of tiny stars
is that she is fed and dry and happily ours —
my daughter's eyes are blue as Georgian Bay
and define each wave on a summer's day.

... AND MORE

There are hundreds of other forms, far more than space permits in this anthology. This chapter offers a taste of just a few.

Acrostic

An acrostic makes a vertical word, phrase or sentence with the first letter or word of each consecutive line in a poem. The poem can be any length and in any form, and is not necessarily rhymed or metered. In Maxianne Berger's "Constrained Response," for example, the first letter of each line spells out the poem's dedication "For Christian Bök," while in Stephen Scobie's "Queen Mary, She's My Friend," the first words make up the refrain from Bob Dylan's song, "Blowing in the Wind."

Anglo-Saxon

The earliest known English poetry (750-1100 A.D.) was in Anglo-Saxon, an older form of the language so different from what we speak today it must be translated to be understood. It was accentual verse with four strong accents to a line. There was a pause (caesura) in the middle with two strong accents on either side. In each of the resulting half-lines the accented and unaccented syllables were arranged according to five possible patterns. In all cases, one or both of the accented syllables in the first half-line began with the same sound (alliteration) as the first accented syllable after the caesura. This was the only alliterated syllable in the second half-line. When the alliteration was based on consonants the sounds had to be exactly alike, but when based on vowels the sounds did not have to match, as in the different sounding o's in "Obsessive, off-the-wall ‖ opus has received" (line 2 of Maxianne Berger's "Constrained Response"). An example of a line alliterating only one accented syllable in the first half-line is: "one *m*ade to wear ‖ a *m*antle of fire" from Jon Furberg's "Blōdmōnath" (which veers into and out of a strict application of the form). In this excerpt, the underlined words are the strongly accented syllables and the alliterated sound is "m."

Limerick

The limerick, an English folk form derived from the madsong (any song sung by a fool), is a popular — often bawdy — type of light verse. As Alan Wilson's "Particle Limericks" show, however, its intrinsic invitation to humour also offers poets a light-hearted way to tackle more serious subjects, so it makes sense that there is a tradition of using the limerick to write about science. The final punch line is sometimes a variation of line 1. The standard form is straightforward — a five-line stanza consisting of a regular pattern of iambs and anapests rhyming *aabba*. Lines 1, 2 and 5 have three strong accents ("There was | a neutri | no from Kent,") and lines 3 and 4 have two ("Without | any mass"). (A madsong stanza has the same metre but rhymes *abccb*.)

Lipogram

The lipogram, one of the best known techniques developed by the Oulipo[21] movement, is a composition that excludes the use of one or more letters. Christian Bök's lipogram, for instance, uses only the vowel "e." (The poem is from "Chapter E" of Bök's *Eunoia*, where each chapter consists of poems restricted to words with only one of the five vowels.) Nancy Mattson's "Her Other Language" is bleakly appropriate to its subject matter — a woman's inability to speak clearly after a beating — omitting the letters *b*, *f*, *m*, *p* and *v* (labials, fricatives and plosives) that, to be spoken, require the lips to touch.

21　Oulipo is an experimental, avant-garde group of writers who invent their own literary forms. The group was formed in 1960, when ten mathematicians and artists (some with connections to the Surrealists) came together in France. Eventually, they called themselves Ouvroir de littérature potentielle (Oulipo; roughly translated, the name in English is "Workshop for Potential Literature").

Visual

Almost all cultures have a tradition of merging sound — the spoken quality of poems — into shape, to highlight the physical qualities of language. A visual poem is "drawn" on the page to depict the thing it describes and reinforce meaning. Visual poetry has many names (with small differences in definition), including concrete, shaped, pattern, spatial and calligramme. In *poetic designs*, Stephen Adams makes a useful distinction between "shaped" poems — which have a particular visual layout but, like Frances Boyle's "Hand Game," are still to be read; and "visual" poems, which are still made up of letters but that, like art, are primarily meant to be looked at. An example is bp Nichol's "Blues" where, by laying out the word "love" in various patterns and leaving it at that, we are free to speculate on the "evol"utions of love, its ("eeeeeeee") maddening and even its "evol" or dark side. This poem might be saying, "I love in every which way," or "Love turns me upside down and all out of whack, or ..." It has as many interpretations as any piece of visual art.

Douglas Barbour

(b. 1940)

from A FLAME ON THE SPANISH STAIRS: JOHN KEATS IN ROME

I know now I always wanted to write, to
find a way to release the dreams
that spelled desire onto the page
I loved letters from the first for what they
cannot hide — their own palimpsests they
exist in multiple layers of time
without even thinking about it that is what
poetry means to me now   &
without desire nothing's written but   death
eternal to keep us apart.   Oh, there must be
poetry to remember beauty by   & for me at least
half that beauty is your body   flush with
the soul within   but never mine to hold
day or night you are but imagination's grace

———————

Stephen Scobie
(b. 1943)

QUEEN MARY, SHE'S MY FRIEND

The question includes its own
answer: in my beginning is
my end. Remember Queen Mary, making
friends with the headsman's axe. What
is the end? All of her future days,
blowing like smoke from a casual fire
in the forest of her heart.
The axe lifts over Fotheringay. A soft
wind from the north touches her cheek as she climbs
the steps to the scaffold. There is no
answer, she thinks, and no beginning. But where
is all this smoke coming from,
blowing into her eyes? She can't see, not even the block.
"In my end is my beginning."
The axe answers all of her questions.
Wind ruffles the hair of her head as it falls.

———————

Maxianne Berger

(b. 1949)

CONSTRAINED RESPONSE

Flashy and feisty, furious fun, this ostensibly
Obsessive, off-the-wall opus has received
Rich recognition and the rat's reward of censure.

Constipated critics consider its comic heuristics
Hollow and hammy; harangue and ravage its
Robust rap, its rambunctious idiosyncrasies.
"Ill-conceived idea," they insist, with smugness.
"Startling stanzas, but a steel-souled stunt, total
Trickery when taken together." Invective
Intended to insure this "Ingenious affectation," this
"Artful atrocity" will achieve absolute notoriety.
"Nimble nonsense!" "Noisome balladeering!"

Balls! This bestseller's beguiling, an opulent
Oeuvre; and open-minded opinions kibosh those
Know-it-all killjoys with keen kudos for its flash.

———————

Jon Furberg
(1944–1992)

BLŌDMŌNATH

Arms and shoulders   carved with serpents,
waist girdled in bronze   beaten gold —
Odin who named all   healed none:
one knocked down   a spear in his eye,
one made to wear   a mantle of fire,
one a mere head   frowning in mud!

Odin the craftsman   red in the forgelight
raises his hammer   higher than doom
to flash upon the shield of night:
one trying to run   away in the mist
    stops to look down   nothing below his knees,
    dropped with a cry   to Odin the deaf,
    legs blunt stumps   like altar stones
    burned iron, cracked   and half-buried,
    but the animals heard,   hewed him down
    until he stared   straight into heaven
    and the wild dog's ecstasy!

Odin the new field   and the sower,
Odin the spoiled seed   the cry for water:
Odin the one pinned to a tree,   warped, ugly limb,
    the forest afire,   trees gnarled black,
    burls like warts,   deadfalls rolling
    in steaming muck,   nothing to glean;
    here men are hardwood,   human bark
    burns hot and long   smoke grey and sodden!

Men's tongues riddled   but the constant sea
is wide as god's eye;   She lifts and sighs:
Odin the long sun,   longer dark,
Odin the speechless   master of song,
Odin the reaper   and the gatherer:
    Sky bulging and thundering,   bloodswath
    through young, silver wheat   green hay.
    One in a meadow   her thighs stained;
    woman in labour   struck in her belly.
    She is our harvest!

Bring in the weaklings   from all the stock.
It is the month of blood,   the air already
full of the North.   There will be feasting!
"As for our enemies,   we shall leave them
only their eyes,   so they can weep."

Alan Wilson

PARTICLE LIMERICKS

I
There was a neutrino from Kent,
who said, *Why pay any more rent?*
Without any mass,
not even an ass,
I might as well sit in a tent.

2
A drinking electron got tight,
charged randomly into the night,
with a sizzling sound,
he spun to the ground,
and threw up a bundle of light.

3
There was an unstable muon,
who realized something was wrong.
If I don't ditch some mass,
get rid of it fast …
But too late — the muon was gone.

———

Nancy Mattson
(b. 1947)

HER OTHER LANGUAGE

She has had to learn
a language that allows only
words she can say without
the thick skin lines outside
her teeth going anywhere
near each other

in this language the teeth
aching and dry, one cracked
stay a certain distance away

this is her language until
the swelling goes down
days at least

it was his hands that did this

all she can say are ice words
stone words
dust words
tongue-against-the-teeth words
dull sounds through the throat

liquids are all she can swallow
through a thick straw
that hurts when it touches

the slot in her jaw cannot shut
its corners cannot turn
towards her eyes

———————————

Christian Bök
(b. 1966)

from "CHAPTER E"

Greek schemers seek egress *en ténèbres*, then enter the melee — the welter where berserk tempers seethe whenever men's mettle, then men's fettle, gets tested; there, the Greek berserkers sever men's thews, then shred men's flesh. When the rebels beset defended trenches, the defenders retrench themselves, then strengthen the embedded defences. The strengthened deterrence deters the rebels; nevertheless, these men esteem relentlessness; hence, the rebels expend themselves, then reject détente. We see them repel retrenched defencemen, then render the bested men defenceless.

---

bp Nichol
(1944–1988)

BLUES

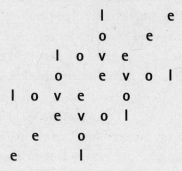

Frances Boyle
(b. 1954)

HAND GAME

               To
             hitch
            a ride
          on what
         it means,
        a word
      here and
    there. Then the exposition, the point of it all comes in
guns blazing and tries to tell the story, clear and complete.
But at the centre, in the palm, no need
to make sense of absolutely everything.
Another reaches out trying for freshness, just wants sometimes
to let it be rude or make a great gesture that only says one thing.
Here is the heartline, the hollow that
Holds the most authentic part of you.
There's a ring of romanticism to the next one over, it lets
you tell the story, how you met someone and wooed him.
No manipulation to handle well
    what folds over itself into a fist.
     You see the strength in what can curl up tiny
      and weak but forms a part of the larger whole.

NOTES TO THE POEMS

"Back on the Job" by John G. Fisher: *The Tribune* in Toronto introduced this poem with: "The following original lines are reproduced in *The Tribune* at the request of Mr. Frank J. Crofton. They were penned by John G. Fisher, a veteran member of the Glass Blowers' Association, who returned to active work in the trade recently, after an absence of about 20 years" (quoted from *The Poetry of the Canadian People 1720-1920: Two Hundred Years of Hard Work*, edited by N. Brian Davis, Toronto: NC Press Ltd., 1976, p. 175).

"The Grey Rider" by Norah M. Holland: In her book, *Spun-Yarn and Spindrift*, Holland says that *Shee* and *Sidhe* mean "fairies"; *Vanathee* means "woman of the house."

"Metric Blues" by F. R. Scott: *Lhude* means loud. The term is used by Ezra Pound in "Ancient Music" ("Winter is icummen in, / Lhude sing Goddamm." Pound's poem is a parody of the anonymous Anglo-Saxon madsong, "Cuckoo Song" (c. 1250) which begins: "Sumer is icumen in, / Lhude sing cuccu!"

"Egg-and-Dart" by Robert Finch: *Egg-and-dart* is a classic architectural design that alternates oval and arrow shapes in a continuous pattern.

"Bugs" (anon): *Paris green* is an insecticide made of copper acetate and arsenic trioxide.

"Quodlibets" by Robert Hayman: In the anthology *The Poets of Canada*, editor John Robert Colombo says this is the first original verse published on the North American continent and notes that "a *quodlibet* (Latin for 'what it pleases') is a debating point" (pp. 25-26). Musically, the quodlibet is defined by Penguin's *A New Dictionary of Music* as a "piece containing several popular tunes put together in unusual and (usually) ingenious fashion —

such as that which ends Bach's 'Goldberg Variations,' incorporating two well-known tunes of his day."

"Sunday Water" by Phyllis Webb: *Wah* refers to Canadian poet Fred Wah.

"Ghazal V" by Kuldip Gill: In her book, *Dharma Rasa*, Gill provides the following translations: *doria*: "decorative wool or cotton extensions for braids;" *baisaki*: "spring festival;" *gulabi*: "rose colour;" *khoti*: "a small room, sometimes on a rooftop;" *doli*: "very sad wedding songs, also the cart that carries a bride away" (pp. 101-103).

"IX" from *Stilt Jack* by John Thompson: *Captain Kangaroo*, a popular educational program for young children, was the longest running television show in history. Bob Keeshan, who also played the role of Clarabell the Clown on the *Howdy Doody Show*, was the gentle Captain Kangaroo (named for all his many pockets) who appeared on TV every weekday morning from 1955–1984. "Smokin' cigarettes and watchin' Captain Kangaroo" is a line from the song "Flowers on the Wall," written by the Statler Brothers, that featured these lines from the chorus, "Playin' solitaire 'til dawn with a deck of fifty-one / Smokin' cigarettes and watchin' Captain Kangaroo / Now don't tell me I've a-nothin' to do."

A Linen Crow, A Caftan Magpie by Patrick Lane: Lane notes, at the end of this book, that the "… form is not the ghazal though I deluded myself for a time thinking it was. It is rather a composite of the haiku and ghazal, a resemblance and nothing more, perhaps more oriental than occidental."

"Excellence in the small. Tears frozen on your face" by Lorna Crozier: The title of this poem, like others in "The Book of Praise" (from Crozier's *Apocrypha of Light*), is a line from Patrick Lane's book of poetry *A Linen Crow, A Caftan Magpie*.

"Revelation" by Aaron Pope and Jodi A. Shaw: Pope and Shaw explain that this poem "is an excerpt from an (as yet) unpublished collaborative long-poem composed in forms (sonnets, ghazals, haiku, glosas, etc.) in honour of, and in response to, the life and work of the late John Thompson. The collaboration took place over a span of four months by e-mail, volleying either line-by-line, stanza-by-stanza, or poem-by-poem" (in correspondence with the editors).

"Shouting Your Name Down the Well" by David W. McFadden: David McFadden says that the title of his sequence refers to a Japanese tradition that the spirit of the recently deceased can sometimes be called back to earth by shouting their name down the well (in correspondence with the editors). "Takuboku" refers to the Japanese poet Ishikawa Takuboku (1886–1912). William J. Higginson, in *The Haiku Handbook*, says Takuboku's work strongly influenced modern tanka and that he "did not care whether he limited himself to the nominal thirty-one-sound length of traditional tanka. Yet almost all of his tanka actually contain the traditional meters or a close approximation to them."

"Leafsmoke" by Marianne Bluger: *my friend Diana* refers to Canadian poet Diana Brebner.

"Hymn for Portia White" by George Elliot Clarke: *Portia White* (1911-1968) was a classical singer and brilliant interpreter of black spirituals. Of Africadian (African-Acadian) descent, she was born in Truro, Nova Scotia, the third of thirteen children. Her father, the descendant of slaves and an ordained minister, was the first black student to graduate from Acadia University. As the family was very poor, the community (including the mayor of Halifax, the president of the Halifax Ladies' Musical Club and the lieutenant-governor), set up and contributed to the Nova Scotia Talent Trust, created in 1944 to support White's early musical training and later singing career. The trust still exists to support young artists.

"To Lighten Heavy Loads" by Aua: This is among the Inuit songs collected and translated by Danish explorer Knud Rasmussen, who included them in his *Report of the Fifth Thule Expedition*, *1921-1924*. In his introduction to *Poems of the Inuit*, John Robert Colombo notes that "The Inuktitut word for breath, *anerca*, also means poetry" (p. 14). He quotes Rasmussen on "To Lighten

Heavy Loads": "Aua himself had, as a young man, learnt certain charms of this sort from an old woman named Qeqertuanaq, in whose family they had been handed down from generation to generation dating back to 'the very first people on earth.' And by way of payment Aua had undertaken to feed and clothe her for the rest of her life. They had always to be uttered in her name, or they would be of no avail" (p. 111).

"Autochthon" by Sir Charles G. D. Roberts: *Autochthon* means those who are indigenous to a given place, said to have been born of the very earth where they reside; hence Aboriginal people. In Greece, the Athenians, in particular, adopted the title for themselves.

"Nightspell" by John Furberg: In his note to this poem in *Anhaga*, Furberg says: "Related to our idea of spelling — the right runes in the right order. One who knows how to spell possesses magical powers. The Anglo-Saxons believed that eloquence generated force beyond physical strength, and charms were serious invocations. By chanting from a high place, a priest might dumbfound and incapacitate an enemy. A spell could be made either to cause or to prevent harm" (p. 75).

"Spell for a Daughter" by Theresa Kishkan: Kishkan says, "The spell worked. Angelica Alba Pass was born September 13, 1985" (in correspondence with the editors).

"Morenz" by Tim Bowling: Howie *Morenz* (1902-1937) is widely considered the National Hockey League's first superstar. Morenz, whose speed and puck handling were legendary, was known variously as the "streak on skates," "the Stratford streak," and the "Canadien Comet." He spent twelve of his fourteen years in the NHL (1923-1937) with the Montreal Canadiens, scoring just over 290 career goals in that league (in 1929-30, he scored an amazing 40 goals in 44 games). He died suddenly a few weeks after breaking his leg during an NHL game at the Montreal Forum, as a result of complications related to the injury. A three-time Hart Trophy winner, Morenz was one of the first players to be elected to the Hockey Hall of Fame when it was created in 1945.

"His Flute, My Ears" by Gregory Scofield: The final stanza in this poem closes with a translation of the Cree phrases.

"Empty Chairs" by Maxianne Berger: Berger says, "This pantoum varies from 'traditional' format in that the repeatons are changed: altered through polyptotonic variation to play on the contrasts set up by the poem's premise" (in correspondence with the editors).

"Forecast, Nadja" by Susan Elmslie: In 1926 in Paris, Andre Breton met a woman named Nadja who personified for him the mysterious, unknowable "woman." Based on their brief, intense affair, he published a surrealist romance about her, titled *Nadja*. Very little outside Breton's book is known about her, except that shortly after their affair, Nadja was hospitalized for erratic behaviour. She spent time at the Sainte-Anne and Perray-Vaucluse mental hospitals before being moved to another, closer to her family in Lille, where she died in 1941. Elmslie discusses her manuscript of poems related to Nadja in an essay, "Trailing Nadja: On Writing *I Nadja, and Other Poems*," in *Poetics.ca* #3 (at www.poetics.ca/elmslie.html). "Forecast, Nadja" is also a dramatic monologue — i.e., a poem written in a character's words, which, as they unfold, reveal time, place and circumstance (including other characters) as well as the speaker's nature.

"The Edge" by Fred Cogswell: *loup-garou* means werewolf.

"The King's Sabbath" by Archibald Lampman: Lampman's sonnet retells the story of Norway's King Olaf (995-1030) who burned his hand to show "he would hold fast by God's law and commandment, and not trespass without punishment on what he knew to be right." (ref.: chapter 201, part VII of the "Saga of Olaf Haraldson (St. Olaf)," in Snorri Sturluson's *Heimskringla*, translated by Samuel Laing, London, 1844). Olaf was noted for his cruelty and for using force to convert the Norwegians to Christianity. He ruled for fifteen years, but fled to Russia in 1029 when the people revolted against him and the nobles sided with the invading Knut the Great. Olaf returned and attempted to regain his throne in 1030 but was killed at the battle of Stiklestad. Pope Alexander III canonized Olaf in 1164, his cruelty forgotten in favour of his services to the church. Sturluson's saga recounts tales of Olaf's healing powers, and miracles are said to occur at his tomb. (Olave is a variant of the name Olaf; references to this period frequently use Dane, Norwegian and Scandinavian interchangeably.)

"Low Tide at Grand Pré" by Bliss Carman: Acadie refers to Acadia, the areas in what is now New Brunswick and Nova Scotia that were settled by the French in the seventeenth and eighteenth centuries. Grand Pré is the site of Longfellow's romantic poem "Evangeline," based on Le Grand Dérangement, the name given by the Acadians to their tragic expulsion from the country by the British in 1755. The exiles were allowed to return after New France was ceded to England in 1763. Most of today's Acadians live in New Brunswick, Nova Scotia and Prince Edward Island as well as parts of Quebec and Maine.

"Coming Up for Air" by David Waltner-Toews: Waltner-Toews says, "This poem is from a sequence of five terzanelles and a sonnet written from the point of view of an ultralight, and dedicated to Carl Hiebert, who took me up with him. Confined to a wheelchair since 1971, Carl flew his open-cockpit ultralight aircraft 5,000 miles across Canada, landing at Expo '86 in Vancouver. The five elements in the Chinese calendar are earth, metal, water, wood and fire. The Greek tradition had earth, air, fire and water. I have amalgamated the two groups" (in correspondence with the editors).

"A Flame on the Spanish Stairs: John Keats in Rome" by Douglas Barbour: The acrostic on the first word of each line forms a phrase from Keats' letters.

"Queen Mary, She's My Friend" by Stephen Scobie: The acrostic is on the first word of each line, which forms the refrain from Bob Dylan's "Blowing in the Wind."

"Blōdmōnath" by Jon Furberg: Furberg says in his introduction to *anhaga*, from which this poem is taken, that "the book is a gathering of poems that emerged during an attempt to make a conventional translation of the Anglo-Saxon elegy, *The Wanderer*." In the process, however, he found himself "embarked on a work not of translation, but of imagination and correspon-dence ..." Most poems are in free verse, but a couple, like this one, more closely follow the Anglo-Saxon alliterative verse form.

COMING TO TERMS

Prosody is the study of the technical devices of form — especially line, metre (and rhythm), repetition and rhyme — that, together, make poetry distinct from prose. The word is derived from the Latin, *prosodia*, which refers to the accents on syllables — hardly surprising, given the central importance of accent and metre in poetry until the advent of free verse in the twentieth century. Of course many of these techniques are also useful — even vital — for the free verse poet, but here we will focus only on their use in formal poetry.

We have divided this section into four parts, each addressing one of the above devices. For ease of reference, the terms here, along with those used in the chapter introductions, are also listed in the index.

We have used standard poetic notation: metre is indicated by a line under strongly accented syllables; feet are indicated by a single vertical line; caesurae by a double vertical line; line breaks by a slash; stanza breaks by a double slash; and rhyming sounds or words in the section on rhyme by italics. Soft accents on a word are indicated by ˘ and strong accents by ´. In rhyme patterns, such as $abbAB^1B^2$ in the madrigal, capital letters stand for the repeated refrain, and numbered capitals — B^1B^2 — indicate rhymed, but otherwise different, refrain lines.

Line

One key distinction between prose and poetry is that the latter (with the possible exception of the prose poem) is based on the line rather than the paragraph. Moreover, the line acts somewhat like a conductor's baton, in that it draws together all the other elements — including rhyme, metre and repetition — to complete the poem's overall music; even visual poems like Frances Boyle's "Hand Game" rely on this key element to create its shape and impact.

A poem's tone, pace, meaning and emotion are all influenced by its lines — whether they are long or short; where they break in relation to syntax; how they interact with phrases, sentences and stanzas; the way they end in relation to rhyme and metre (e.g. softly with an unstressed syllable, emphatically with a stressed rhyme) and so on. The following are some devices involved in constructing the poetic line.

CAESURA: From the Latin for "cutting," a caesura (also spelled cesura) is a pause marking the natural rhythms of speech in a line of poetry. Usually near the middle of the line, it is often indicated by punctuation, as in "I embrace everything, || even the slither of midnight" from Sina Queyras' "Tonight the Sky Is My Begging Bowl."

END STOPPED: A line of poetry in which grammar and sense are complete (i.e., not carried over to the following line), so the reader naturally pauses before reading on. Often signified by a punctuation mark. For example, the following lines in Jay Macpherson's "The Third Eye" are end-stopped: "Of three eyes, I would still give two for one. / The third eye clouds: its light is nearly gone."

ENJAMBED: A phrase or sentence that is not complete in one line and must be carried over to the next, as in the following from Sir Charles G. D. Roberts' "The Skater": "Till the startled hollows awoke and heard // A spinning whisper, a sibilant twang."

HETEROMETRIC: Stanzas with lines that have different meters. For example, see Annie Charlotte Dalton's "The Praying Mantis," where lines one and two of each stanza have four strong accents and lines three and four have three.

INDENTATION: Often used to indicate a slight pause in reading or to suggest a change in rhyme scheme; for instance if four lines are rhymed *abab*, the *b* lines may be indented. Indentation may also indicate different metres. John McRae gives the *b* rhymed lines a slight indentation, and the unrhymed refrain lines a larger indentation, in his rondeau, "In Flanders Fields."

ISOMETRIC: Stanzas with all lines in the same metre. For example, see Margaret Avison's "Tennis," where each line is in iambic pentameter. Mark Strand and Eavan Boland in *The Making of a Poem* point out that isometric poetry was the norm until the end of the Middle Ages, when poets began to experiment with varying line lengths.

PARENTHESIS: Parenthesis in the poetic line is used to indicate an aside or insert information without disrupting the overall syntax. Its mild interruption offers a succinct way to add depth and complexity to content, particularly when the option of going off on a tangent would intrude on what is being said. Glenn Kletke uses this throughout "O Grandfather Dust." In these lines, for instance, the device adds descriptive detail to a list: "... pail / of well water (cold, so cold) , tin dipper, sky dipper, Milky Way." And it adds emotional emphasis, a whiff of death, in the lines: "... how later in the morning you would carry to her / (O grandmother ashes!) prairie smoke ..."

STANZA NAMES

Traditionally, stanzas are named for the number of lines they contain:

- Two lines: couplet
- Three lines: tercet (or triplet if rhyming *aaa*)
- Four lines: quatrain
- Five lines: quintet (or quintain)
- Six lines: sestet
- Seven lines: septet
- Eight lines: octet

Metre

The English language is rich in the number of systems it has for finding the metre — the measure — in a line of poetry. The five systems are: accentual (a pattern based on accents only, as in Anglo-Saxon); syllabic (a pattern based on the number of syllables only, as in haiku); accentual-syllabic (the most common, a combination of both accent and syllable, as in iambic pentameter); quantitative (an adaptation of Greek and Latin metres to English); and free verse (the absence of any regular pattern).

For a detailed explanation of metre, readers can explore the references listed in the bibliography. Very briefly, metrical patterns are divided into "feet." If syllables are like notes of music, then the "foot" is the bar sign that helps us locate ourselves in the patterns we're writing or reading.

Most feet have just one strong accent plus whatever soft accents it needs to complete its pattern. (Examples in this book separate the feet with a vertical line and indicate strongly accented syllables with an underline). There are four primary feet for measuring metre, all based on the concept that each syllable in English has a certain amount of emphasis, or accent, when it's spoken. These are: the iamb (a soft/strong accent as in be-stow), trochee (strong/soft as in ho-ly), anapest (soft/soft/strong as in un-der-stand), and dactyl (strong/soft/soft as in won-der-ful). Others that appear regularly are listed in the definitions below.

Usually the overall pattern is the truest gauge of a poem's metre. To "scan" a poem is to read or analyze its metric pattern (scan comes from the Latin *scandere*, to climb, which rightly suggests that scanning is not always an easy stroll). But poetry is nothing if not flexible, and often a poem's pattern leaves itself open to interpretation. Even the experts can hold widely varying views and sometimes passionately debate the "proper" way to scan certain feet or lines. In the end, the point isn't to debate which is the "right" or "wrong" way to scan a particular poem, but rather, simply to use metre as a tool to enjoy the music of poetry.

Metrical patterns create the underlying beat behind the rhythm of words and lines, while the rhythm of the voice as it reads a line of poetry is often quite different from the poem's metre. Metre is the bass line, the metronome; it clacks along a line regardless of sense. Rhythm is the way we speak — it is tone, inflection, intent. It is the interplay and tension between these two — metre and vocal rhythm — that creates much of the complex beauty of metred forms.

Below are the definitions of several terms related to metre.

METRICAL PATTERNS

There are two main schools of thought regarding how to scan for metre. One shares Robert Frost's view that there are only two kinds of English foot, iambic and loose iambic; the other maintains that a wider range of feet are necessary to accurately depict a poem's metre. By that school's definition, and in order to give the reader as broad a range of terms as possible, the following are the most common feet in English poetry.

AMPHIBRACH: A three-syllable foot, with the strong accent in the middle,
(˘ ´ ˘) flanked by two softly accented syllables. For example, in F. R. Scott's "Metric Blues," the line "The met | ric tal | on's got | you gallon" can be scanned as three iambs and an amphibrach. The last foot could also be scanned as an iamb with a tag.

AMPHIMACER: A three-syllable foot, with two strong accents flanking a softly
(´ ˘ ´) accented syllable. To use F. R. Scott's "Metric Blues" again (see amphibrach), the pattern throughout the poem suggests these one-foot lines are amphimacers: "Yell and flinch / ell and inch."

ANAPEST: A three-syllable foot, with the strong accent on the third. It
(˘ ˘ ´) often provides a light, speedy, rhythm to a line, as in Richard Outram's "Tourist Stricken At the Uffizi," where even the commas and the iambic feet can't slow the rush of the four anapestic feet: "Dear God, | for the rest | of my life; / And how | shall I tell | her, my wife."

CATALECTIC: A final metrical foot in a line that, based on the prevailing
(´) pattern of metre in the poem, is incomplete. In "Cathleen Sweeping," George Johnston mainly uses iambic feet, but frequently substitutes a trochee for variety. So, in this poem, the additional accented syllable at the end of a line could make the final foot catalectic: "She sweeps | against | the cold | clumsy | sky.") The final two feet could also be read as a single amphimacer.

DACTYL: A three-syllable foot, with the strong accent on the first.
(´ ˘ ˘) Marjorie Pickthall opens the following line from "Ebb Tide" with two dactyls: "Borne from the | fight and the | full en | deavour."

IAMB: A two-syllable foot with the strong accent on the second.
(˘ ´) For example, the following line from Annie Charlotte Dalton's "The Praying-Mantis" has four iambs: "Strange crea | tures walk | and breed | their kind."

PYRRHIC: (˘ ˘)	A foot consisting of two softly accented syllables, it usually appears with a spondee, as in the line, "The <u>break</u>, | the <u>cast</u>, | the <u>fe</u> | ver, the | <u>held</u> <u>breath</u>" in Tim Bowling's "Morenz."
SPONDEE: (ˉ ˉ)	A foot consisting of two strong accents, usually used for emphasis, as in the first of these two lines from F. R. Scott's "Metric Blues": "<u>Frown</u>, <u>pound</u>, / you're <u>quite</u> un<u>sound</u>."
TAG: (˘)	A soft accent at the end of a metered line, that allows for colloquial speech. The tag is counted as part of the last foot. For example, the anonymous "Bugs" alternates iambic trimeter and tetrameter lines and every trimeter line ends with a tag. In the final line, "That <u>eats</u> | with<u>out</u> | per<u>mis</u>sion," the tag is the final (softly accented) syllable, "sion," and is considered part of the final iambic foot. Alternatively, this foot could be called an amphibrach.
TROCHEE: (´ ˘)	A two-syllable foot, with the strong accent on the first. For example, the following line from Marilyn Bowering's "Widow's Winter" has four trochees: "<u>Christ</u>, my |<u>heart's</u> a | <u>bit</u>ter | <u>sin</u>ner."

Poets often use a technique called substitution to give variety and the power of the unexpected to regularly metred lines.

SUBSTITUTION:	The prevailing metrical pattern is often varied by substituting a different foot for the one generally used. This can be very powerful, as in P.K. Page's "Water and Marble." Page writes in an overall iambic pattern as the speaker talks about the power of her lover, as in the line: "and <u>when</u> | his <u>name</u> | is <u>spo</u> | ken <u>pale</u> | still <u>sky</u>"). Occasionally, though, she opens a line with a trochee, breaking the iambic pattern, as in "<u>trem</u>bles | and <u>breaks</u> | and <u>moves</u> …" Just as the speaker trembles, so the pattern trembles, too, and almost breaks — sound and sense, powerfully working together.

Repetition

Repetition is used in a variety of ways, particularly to intensify emotion in poetry. It can build suspense, add emphasis, suggest inevitability, exhibit obsessiveness and so on. There are seemingly countless technical terms for this device, each denoting a different type of recurrence for words, lines, phrases, sentences and stanzas. Some of the most commonly used are described below.

(Repetition also provides the foundation for a number of fixed forms, including the fugue, ghazal, glosa, madrigal, palindrome, pantoum, rondeau, rondel, roundel, roundelay, sestina, terzanelle, triolet and villanelle; how it is employed in those forms is discussed in the various introductions.)

REFRAIN

"Refrain" is often broadly used to refer to any regularly repeated line(s) that provide a chorus effect in a poem. However, refrain is one of several terms that have more precise meanings:

BURDEN: A complete stanza that is repeated regularly throughout a poem, as in Ryan Knighton's "Ballad of Echolocation."

INCREMENTAL REPETITION: Complete stanzas that are repeated, but with significant alterations each time they appear; the changes, as they accrue, help to build the poem's emotion and give it momentum, as in Bliss Carman's ballad, "Buie Annajohn."

REFRAIN:	Part of one stanza that is regularly repeated in each successive stanza. For example, the lines "Grey Rider of the Shee?" and "To-night, O Vanathee" in Norah M. Holland's "The Grey Rider" are refrains. (Sometimes also used synonymously with "burden" and "repetend.")
REPETEND:	A line or phrase that is irregularly repeated, sometimes with variations, throughout a poem. The lines "And the season advances" in Herménégilde Chiasson's fugue of the same title, and "They do not get very far in a day" in Robyn Sarah's "Fugue," are repetends.

WORDS AND PHRASES

ANADIPLOSIS:	A word or phrase used at the end of one line and repeated at the beginning of the next. For example, the word "dead" in the first two lines of A.J.M. Smith's "News of the Phoenix": "They say the Phoenix is dying, some say dead / Dead without issue is what one message said."
ANAPHORA:	Word(s) repeated at the beginning of consecutive lines. For example, "I jab my tools in water / I jab them in charcoal, / I jab them at the bottle's neck" from John G. Fisher's "Back on the Job." Used persistently throughout a poem, this device has an incantatory effect, as in Penny Kemp's "Bidding Spell."
	Anaphora also refers to this kind of repetition *within* lines when the word(s) start successive phrases or sentences. For example, the phrase "dead in" at the beginning and in the middle of most lines in Thuong Vuong-Riddick's "My Beloved is Dead in Vietnam."
EPANALEPSIS:	Use of the same word(s) at both the beginning and the end of a single line, as in E.J. Pratt's "The Lee-Shore": "Keep away from the land, keep away."
EPISTROPHE:	Word(s) repeated at the end of consecutive lines. For example, the word "marble" ends the last four lines of P.K. Page's "Water and Marble": "… in a dome of marble / and winter seals its floury drifts in marble / all matter double-locks as dense as marble / and I, in other's eyes, am cut from marble."

Epistrophe also refers to this kind of repetition *within* lines when the word(s) end successive phrases and sentences. For example, in stanza 2 of "Fugue," Robyn Sarah ends these two sentences with the word "children": "… They are taking / it all with them: rugs, / pianos, children. Or they are leaving / it all behind them: cats, / plants, children."

EPIZEUXIS: Insistent, multiple repetition of the same word or phrase within a line, often to add emotional intensity, as in "This beating, beating, beating of the heart" from Robert Finch's "Egg and Dart," and "Yeats. Yeats. Yeats. Yeats. Yeats. Yeats." from John Thompson's ghazal "IX."

ITERATIO: A word or phrase repeated only once, without interruption, within a line. Zachariah Wells uses this to convey a resigned humour in "Fool's Errand": "… they'll freeze to death / Out there. Out there then I went." Kenneth Leslie, on the other hand, uses it to achieve a thoughtful tone in line two of "Sonnet": "silver of life, life's silver sheen of glory."

POLYPTOTON: A word repeated almost immediately but in a different form, as in "Why are you most happy when happiness fails?" from Patrick Lane's ghazal in *A Linen Crow, A Caftan Magpie*.

SYMPLOCE: Repetition at both the beginning and end of successive lines, where the word(s) at the start are different from those at the end. Tim Bowling uses this device in lines one and two of "Morenz": "The crowds, the cheers, the broken leg, the death. / The crowds, the tears, the open casket, the death."

Rhyme

A central feature of most form poetry, rhyme is the matching of like sounds in words. It occurs not only at the ends of lines, but within them.

For centuries, its detractors have condemned rhyme for much the same reasons as John Milton did in his defence of using blank verse (unrhymed iambic pentameter lines) in "Paradise Lost." In his preface to that poem, Milton called rhyme "the invention of a barbarous age, to set off wretched matter and lame metre;" and argued that "true musical delight … consists only in apt numbers, fit quantity of syllables, and the sense variously drawn out from one verse into another, not in the jingling sound of like endings …"[23]

Of course, Milton knew a good rhyme when he saw one, and used the device well in numerous poems. His argument was against poor rhyme, the kind that "jingles." Handled well, rhyme does not have to intrude or distract. As Alexander Pope said in his *An Essay on Criticism*, "The sound must seem an echo to the sense." And when that is the case, rhyme can profoundly influence the music, tone and emotional impact of a poem. Rhyme schemes play a role in how stanzaic poems are structured — once established, they tend to be repeated throughout, as in the *ababab* pattern of Zachariah Wells' "Fool's Errand."

Rhyme is usually categorized by its sound and its position in words, lines and stanzas. Rhyming sounds or words in the examples that follow are indicated by italics.

SOUND

ALLITERATION: Repetition of initial sounds of words in close proximity, for example, the letter *b* in this line from Leonard Cohen's "Twelve O'Clock Chant": "In *b*urlap *b*ags the *b*ankers sew me." Alliteration is also a structuring element in Anglo-Saxon poetry (see the last chapter). (Also called head and initial rhyme)

ASSONANCE: Repetition of vowels that sound the same in words, for example, the letter *i* in "… beh*i*nd us. We arr*i*ve" in Diana Brebner's "The Golden Lotus."

CONSONANCE: Repetition of consonants that sound the same in words, for example, the letter *l* in "Come*l*y and s*l*ender?" in Irving Layton's "Song for Naomi."

EYE: An exception to rhyme based on sound, this is based on the spelling of words; i.e., they look similar but sound different. For example, *blood* and *mood* at the end of lines one and two in Bliss Carman's "Vagabond Song" and *breath* and *wreath* in Zachariah Wells' "Fool's Errand." In many cases eye-rhymes likely sounded alike at one point, but lost that quality over the years as pronunciations changed.

---

23   Milton, John. *Paradise Lost and Other Poems*. Markham: Penguin Books Canada, 1981, p. 34.

FULL:	Words where, as Edward Hirsch says in *How to Read a Poem*, "initial sounds are different and all succeeding sounds are identical;" for example, l*awn* and y*awn* in Anne Simpson's "Waking" or t*ower* and p*ower* in Archibald Lampman's "The City of the End of Things" (also called perfect, true and pure rhyme).
IDENTICAL:	Rhyming by repeating the same word; for example Bliss Carman uses identical rhyme in lines 2 and 5 throughout "Low Tide on Grand Pré." Identical rhyme is one of the traditional elements for the second line of each ghazal couplet.
MACARONIC:	The rhyming of words from different languages, for example, *lire* and *hear* in Herménégilde Chiasson's sonnet, "Appollo at Aberdeen."
NEAR:	Words that sound different but contain some of the same sounds, giving more of an echo than a full rhyme; for example, do*or* and we*re* in Stephen Heighton's "Blackjack." Usually these rhymes rely on assonance or consonance (also called approximate, half, imperfect, off, oblique and slant rhyme).
ONOMATOPOEIA:	Words that make the sound of what they stand for; for example, *Buzzin'* in George Elliot Clarke's "King Bee Blues": "I'm an ol' king bee, honey, / Buzzin' from flower to flower."
RICH RHYME:	Words that sound exactly the same, but are spelled differently and have different meanings (i.e., homophones); for example, the end rhyme in Phyllis Webb's "The Second Hand": "tying our hearts in a lover's *knot*; // now, whether we flower or *not*" (from the French term, *rime riche*).

POSITION IN WORDS

ONE-SYLLABLE:	Words that rhyme on the final strongly accented syllable in the line, as in *mouse*, *grouse* and *house* in Glenn Kletke's "O Grandfather Dust" or ob*scure* and im*mure* in Margaret Avison's "Rondeau Redoublé" (also called masculine rhyme).

TWO-SYLLABLE: Words that rhyme across two syllables, including on the soft accent that ends a line; for example, *wonder* and *thunder* in Marjorie Pickthall's "Ebb Tide (also called *feminine* or *double* rhyme).

TRIPLE RHYME: Words that rhyme across three syllables, as in vulg*arity* and cl*arity* in Sharon Thesen's "The Broken Cup."

APOCOPATED: The final syllable of one of the words is left out of the rhyme; for example, *sleep*ing and *sweep* in Marilyn Bowering's "Autobiography."

BROKEN: More than one word is used to complete the rhyme; for example, V*enus* and betw*een us* in Richard Outram's "Tourist Stricken at the Uffizi" (also called *mosaic* rhyme).

WRENCHED: The strongly accented syllable of one word rhymes with a softly accented syllable in another; for example, gl*ow* and furr*ow* in Daniel David Moses' "Fall;" *fur* and hamburg*er* in George McWhirter's "An Era of Easy Meat at Locarno."

POSITION IN LINES

END: Any instance where the rhyme falls on the last word in lines (also called terminal rhyme).

INTERNAL: Rhyme within a line; for example, "A pal's last n*eed* is a thing to h*eed*, so I swore I would not fail" in Robert Service's "The Cremation of Sam McGee."

CHAIN: The last syllable of one line rhymes with the first syllable in the next, as in the like sounds of the italicized letters in "… had been a bett*er* / b*ir*thingplace than rock …" from Jon Furberg's "Nightspell."

POSITION IN STANZAS (RHYME SCHEMES)

COUPLET: A rhyme scheme where words at the ends of two consecutive lines rhyme (*aa*), as in these lines from Barker Fairely's "Bach Fugue": "This is the first of the themes, the lecturer s*aid*, / Please be at pains to fix it in the h*ead*."

CROSSED: A rhyme scheme where end words of alternate lines rhyme (*abab*), as in the first four lines of Archibald Lampman's

"The City of the End of Things": "Beside the pounding cata*racts* / Of midnight streams unknown to ***us*** / 'Tis builded in the leafless t*racts* / And valleys huge of Tartar***us***" (also called alternating and interlocking rhyme).

ENVELOPE: A rhyme scheme where rhyming end words of two or more lines are enclosed by rhyming words in the line before and after them (*abba*). For example, Pauline Johnson's "The Train Dogs" uses envelope rhyme: "Savage of breed and of b*one*, / Shaggy and swift comes the yelping b***and***, / Freighters of fur from the voiceless l***and*** / That sleeps in the Arctic z*one*." This pattern can be made more complex when there are more than two enclosed lines, only some of which rhyme (*abcba*) (also called inserted rhyme).

INTERMITTENT: A rhyme scheme where only the end words of alternate lines rhyme, as in the ballad stanza (*abcb*); for example, the rhyme scheme in all but the last two lines of John G. Fisher's "Back on the Job": "I jab my tools in water / I jab them in charc*oal*, / I jab them at the bottle's neck, / But there! I've missed the h*ole*."

INTERLACED: A rhyme scheme with two rhymes in consecutive lines — the first rhyme is on words at the mid-line pause (caesura) and the second is on the end words. For example, these lines in Marilyn Bowering's "Widow's Winter": "Bless the r*ed* door open w*ide*. / Bless the d*ead* who play ins*ide*" (also called caesural rhyme).

TERZA RIMA: A particular rhyme scheme for three line stanzas, rhyming *aba bcb cdc*, etc. The envelope in each stanza encloses just one line, which goes on to become the enclosing rhyme in the next stanza.

THORN: An unrhymed line or lines in stanzas that are otherwise rhymed. For example, the unrhymed line 11 in A. M. Klein's "The Still Small Voice."

BIBLIOGRAPHY

Adams, Stephen. *poetic designs: an introduction to meters, verse forms, and figures of speech* (Broadview, 1997; reprinted 2000)

Agha, Shahid Ali, ed. *Ravishing DisUnities, Real Ghazals in English* (Wesleyan University Press, 2000)

Beckson, Karl and Arthur Ganz, eds. *A Reader's Guide to Literary Terms* (The Noonday Press: 1960)

Brogan, T.V.F., ed. *The New Princeton Handbook of Poetic Terms* (Princeton University Press, 1994)

Crozier, Lorna. "Dreaming the Ghazal into Being" in *Bones in Their Wings* (Hagios Press, 2003)

Cuddon, J.A. *A Dictionary of Literary Terms* (Doubleday/Penguin, 1982, revised edition)

Finch, Annie and Kathrine Varnes, eds. *An Exaltation of Forms, Contemporary Poets Celebrate the Diversity of Their Art* (The University of Michigan Press, 2002)

Fuller, John. *The Sonnet* (Methuen, 1972)

Fussell, Paul. *Poetic Meter & Poetic Form* (Random House, 1979, revised edition)

Hecht, Anthony. *Melodies Unheard, Essays on the Mysteries of Poetry* (The Johns Hopkins University Press, 2003)

Higginson, William J., with Penny Harter. *The Haiku Handbook, How to Write, Share, and Teach Haiku* (Kodansha International, 1985)

Hirsch, Edward. *How to Read a Poem — and fall in love with poetry* (A DoubleTake Book, Centre for Documentary Studies, in association with Harvest Books, Harcourt Inc., 1999)

Hirschfield, Jane. *Nine Gates, Entering the Mind of Poetry* (Harper Collins, 1997)

Hollander, John. *Rhyme's Reason* (Yale University Press, 1981)

Holman, C. Hugh. *A Handbook to Literature* (Bobbs-Merrill, 1981, fourth edition)

Lehman, David, ed. *Ecstatic Occasions, Expedient Forms: 65 Leading Contemporary Poets Select and Comment On Their Poems* (MacMillan, 1987)

Matthews, Harry and Alastair Brotchie, eds. *Oulipo Compendium* (Atlas, 1998)

Oliver, Mary. *A Poetry Handbook* (Harcourt Brace, 1994)

_____ , *Rules for the Dance* (Houghton Mifflin, 1998)

Oppenheimer, Paul. *The Birth of the Modern Mind: Self, Consciousness, and the Invention of the Sonnet* (Oxford, 1989)

Packard, William. *The Poets Dictionary* (Harper Perennial, 1994)

Padgett, Ron, ed. *The Teachers and Writers Handbook of Poetic Forms* (Teachers and Writers Collaborative, 1987)

Pinsky, Robert. *The Sound of Poetry, A Brief Guide* (Farrar, Straus and Giroux, 1998)

Skelton, Robin. *The Shapes of Our Singing, A Guide to the Metres and Set Forms of Verse from Around the World* (Eastern Washington University Press, 2002)

Steele, Timothy. *all the fun's in how you say a thing, an explanation of meter and versification* (Ohio University Press, 1999)

Strand, Mark and Eavan Boland, eds. *The Making of a Poem, A Norton Anthology of Poetic Forms* (W.W. Norton and Company, 2000)

Turco, Lewis. *The New Book of Forms, A Handbook of Poetics* (University Press of New England, 1986); and *The Book of Forms, A Handbook of Poetics* (University Press of New England, 2000)

PERMISSIONS

"The Contract Mucker" is reprinted from *The Poetry of the Canadian People 1720-1920: Two Hundred Years of Hard Work*. "Back on the Job" is reprinted from *The Poetry of the Canadian People 1720-1920: Two Hundred Years of Hard Work*. "Buie Annajohn" is reprinted from *The Selected Poems of Bliss Carman*. "The Cremation of Sam McGee" is reprinted with the permission of the Robert Service estate. "The Grey Rider" is reprinted from *Spun-Yarn and Spindrift*. "The Lee-Shore" from *E.J. Pratt: Complete Poems* (Sandra Djwa & R.G. Moyles, eds; 1989) is used with the permission of the E.J. Pratt estate and the publisher, University of Toronto Press Inc. "1838" taken from *The Gods* by Dennis Lee. Used by permission of McClelland & Stewart Ltd. "The Ballad of Echolocation" from *Swing in the Hollow* is used by permission of Anvil Press.

"Conjured" is reprinted from *Album of a Heart*. "Metric Blues" by F.R. Scott is taken from *The Dance is One*. Permission to reprint the poem has been granted by F.R. Scott's literary executor, William Toye. "Who" from *The Curing Berry* is used with the permission of the poet. "Self-Sufficient Blues" from *Why I Sing the Blues* (Jan Zwicky and Brad Cran, eds) is used by permission of Smoking Lung Press and the poet. "The Diet" from *Anywhere* is used by permission of Exile Editions. "King Bee Blues" from *Whylah Falls* is used by permission of Polestar Book Publishers. "Blues" from *Instruments of Surrender* is used by permission of Buschek Books. "Jump Rope Rhyme of the 49er Daughters" and "Alley" from *49th Parallel Psalm* are used by permission of Arsenal Pulp Press, Advance Editions.

"The Skater" is reprinted from *Poems*. "Bach Fugue" from *Wild Geese and Other Poems* by Barker Fairley is reprinted with the permission of the publisher, Penumbra Press. "Egg-and-Dart" from *Poems* by Robert Finch. Copyright 1946 by Oxford University Press Canada. Reprinted by permission of the publisher. "The Third Eye" from *Poems Twice Told* by Jay Macpherson. Copyright 1981 by Oxford University Press Canada. Reprinted by permission of the publisher. "April Elegy" from *Crossing the Salt Flats* is used by permission of Porcupine's Quill. "James Clarence Mangan in Trinity College Library" from *Climbing Croagh Patrick* is used by permission of Oolichan Books. "Jaham Sings of the Fear of the Moon" from *Araby* is used by permission of Signal Editions. "The Fall" from *The White Line* is used by permission of the poet.

Excerpt from *Quodlibets* by Robert Hayman is reprinted from *The Poets of Canada*. "Bugs" is reprinted from *The Poetry of the Canadian People 1720-1920: Two Hundred Years of Hard Work*. "Brebeuf and his Brethren" by F.R. Scott taken from *Collected Poems*. Permission to reprint the poem has been granted by F.R. Scott's literary executor, William Toye. Excerpt from "Four Epigrams" from *Variations and Theme* is used by permission of Porcupine's Quill. "News of the Phoenix" taken from *The Classic Shade, Selected Poems* by A.J.M Smith. Used by permission of McClelland & Stewart Ltd. "Going to Sleep" from *Collected Poems: The Two Seasons* is used by permission of the estate of Dorothy Livesay. "Very Short Poem" by Raymond Souster is reprinted from *Collected Poems of Raymond Souster* by permission of Oberon Press. "Tourist Stricken at the Uffizi" from *Turns & Other Poems* is used by permission of the poet. "Aunt Jane" is used by permission of the estate of Alden Nowlan. "[you fit into me]" from *Power Politics* is used by permission of House of Anansi. Excerpt from "Winter Epigrams" taken from *Winter Epigrams and Epigrams to Ernesto Cardenal in Defense of Claudia* by permission of the poet.

"The Praying Mantis" is reprinted from *Poetry by Canadian Women*. "The Ballad of the Pink-Brown Fence" is reprinted from *I've Tasted My Blood*. "The Children Are Laughing" from *Gwendolyn MacEwan: Volume One, The Early Years* is used by permission of Exile Editions. "And the Season Advances" from *Climates* is used by permission of Goose Lane Editions. "Fugue" from *The Touchstone* is used by permission of House of Anansi. "Night Piece" from *The Edge of Time* is used by permission of Ronsdale Press. "Madrigal, A Lullaby for Xan" from *Love As It Is* is used by permission of Beach Holme Press.

Excerpt from "Sunday Water" from *Water and Light* is used by permission of the poet. "Ghazal V" from *Dharma Rasa* is used by permission of Nightwood Editions. "Stilt Jack IX" from *Stilt Jack* is used by permission of House of Anansi. Excerpt from *A Linen Crow, A Caftan Magpie* is used by permission of Thistledown Press. "Of Night" by Molly Peacock is used by permission of the poet. "Excellence in the small. Tears frozen on your face" taken from *Apocrypha of Light* by Lorna Crozier. Used by permission of McClelland & Stewart. "Tonight the Sky is my Begging Bowl" by Sina Queyras is used by permission of the poet. "Landscapes and home/Ghazal 22" by Yvonne Blomer is used by permission of the poet.

"Planet Earth" from *Planet Earth — Poems Selected & New* is used by permission of Porcupine's Quill. "The Garden Temple" from *A Linen Crow, A Caftan Magpie* is used by permission of Thistledown Press. "O Grandfather Dust" by Glenn Kletke is used by permission of the poet. "Last Days" from *Still* is used by permission of Black Moss Press. "Revelation" by Aaron Pope and Jodi A. Shaw is used by permission of the poets. "What do you want?" by Brenda Leifso is used by permission of the poet. "Norgberto Hernandez — Photographed Falling September Eleventh" by David Reibetanz is used by permission of the poet.

Excerpt from "Spring" from *Even a Stone Breathes: Haiku and Senryu* is used by permission of Oolichan Books. "Tanka" by Henry Beissel is used by permission of the poet. "Father/Mother Haibun #5" from *Waiting for Saskatchewan* is used by permission of Turnstone Press. "Shouting Your Name Down the Well" from *Five Star Planet* is used by permission of Talon Books. "Leafsmoke" from *Tamarack & Clearcut* is used by permission of McGill-Queen's Press. Excerpt from "Hortus Urbanus / Urban Garden" by Colin Morton is used by permission of the poet. "Shuffles" from *The Afterlife of Trees* is used by permission of McGill-Queen's Press. "Hymn for Portia White" from *Blue* is used by permission of Polestar Book Publishers. "Haiku Monument for Washington, D.C." taken from *Asphodel* by Michael Redhill. Used by permission of McClelland & Stewart Ltd. "leavetaking" from *Monkey Puzzle* is used by permission of the poet.

Excerpt from "Magic Words" is reprinted from *Poems of the Inuit*. "Autochthon" is reprinted from *Selected Poems of Sir Charles G.D. Roberts*. "Twelve O'Clock Chant" taken from *The Spice-Box of Earth* by Leonard Cohen. Used by permission of McClelland & Stewart Ltd. "My Beloved is Dead in Vietnam" from *Two Shores / Deux rives* is used by

"Acoustics" from *Science Lessons: Poems* is used by permission of Oolichan Books. "An Era of Easy Meat at Locarno" by George McWhirter is used by permission of the poet. "so'net 3" by Paul Dutton is used by permission of the poet. Excerpt from "Hail: Word Sonnets" by Seymour Mayne is used by permission of the poet. "Head and Torso of the Minotaur" by John Reibetanz is used by permission of the poet. "Apollo at Aberdeen" from *Climates* is used by permission of Goose Lane Editions. "Glenn Gould's Hands" by Kate Braid is used by permission of the poet. "The Golden Lotus" from *The Golden Lotus* is used by permission of Netherlandic Press. "Waking" by Anne Simpson is used by permission of the poet. "For Peter, My Cousin" from *The Gladys Elegies* (1977), published by Coteau Books. Used with the permission of the publisher. "Rural Gothic" by Shane Neilson is used by permission of the poet.

"Drought" is reprinted from *The Poetry of the Canadian People 1720-1920: Two Hundred Years of Hard Work*. "Vagabond Song" is reprinted from *The Selected Poems of Bliss Carman*. "The City of the End of Things" is reprinted from *Canadian Poetry*. "The Train Dogs" is reprinted from *Poetry by Canadian Women*. "Ebb Tide" is reprinted from *Poetry by Canadian Women*. "From the Hazel Bough" taken from *The Poems of Earle Birney* by Earle Birney. Used by permission of McClelland & Stewart Ltd. "Eastern Shore" from *The Mulgrave Road: Selected Poems of Charles Bruce* is used by permission of the poet's estate. "The Still Small Voice" taken from *A.M. Klein: Complete Poems*. Zailig Pollock, editor (University of Toronto Press) 1990. Reprinted with the permission of the publisher. "Water and Marble" from *The Hidden Room: Collected Poems* is used by permission of Porcupine's Quill. "Old Women of Toronto" from *Driving Home* is used by permission of Jonathan Waddington. "The Naked Man" taken from *Salvage* by Michael Crummey. Used by permission of McClelland & Stewart Ltd. "The Conductor" from *Crowd of Sounds* is used by permission of House of Anansi. "Fool's Errand" by Zachariah Wells is used by permission of the poet.

"Death's Head" from *The Works: Collected Poems* is used by permission of the poet. "Round of Life" from *Man in Love* is used by permission of Porcupine's Quill. Excerpt from "The Way Down" from *Poems Twice Told: The Boatman & Welcoming Disaster* by Jay MacPherson. Copyright 1981 by Oxford University Press Canada. Reprinted by permission of the publisher. "Dream Prison" by Barbara Myers is used by permission of the poet. "The Hands" by Daniel David Moses is used by permission of the poet. "The Cherry Laurel" by Russell Thornton is used by permission of the poet. "The Ghost of His Hand" by Nancy Bennett is used by permission of the poet.

"A Night in June" is reprinted from *Poems of Duncan Campbell Scott*. "Tigers Know From Birth" from *The Hangman Ties the Holly* is used by permission of the estate of Anne Wilkinson. "The Second Hand" from *Selected Poems: The Vision Tree* is used by permission of Talonbooks. "In Oak" from *Gathering Wild* is used by permission of Brick Books. "The Broken Cup" from *aurora* is used by permission of the poet. "3. Who was that? I ask" from *Calling Home* is used by permission of Vehicule Press, Signal Editions. "Blackjack" from *The Address Book* is used by permission of House of Anansi.

"Bread to Stone" by Joy Kogawa is used by permission of the poet. "Triolets for Ken" from *Crossing Salt Flats* is used by permission of Porcupine's Quill. "Triolet for the

Amphetamine Afflicted" by Susan McCaslin is used by permission of the poet. "Landing" by Sandy Shreve is used by permission of the poet. "Vuillard Interior" by Elise Partridge is used by permission of the poet. "Night, Hornby Island" by Danielle Janess is used by permission of the poet.

"Catherine Plouffe" is reprinted from *Poetry by Canadian Women*. "The Castle" from *Planet Earth – Poems Selected & New* is used by permission of Porcupine's Quill. "City Park Merry-Go-Round" from *Dreaming Backwards: The Selected Poems of Eli Mandel* is used by permission of Ann Mandel. "Little Miracle" from *Original Love* is used by permission of the poet and W.W. Norton. Excerpt from "Coming Up for Air" by David Waltner-Toews is used by permission of the poet. "Crows" by Carole Glasser Langille is used by permission of the poet. "The Ferry to South Baymouth" from *Anywhere* is used by permission of Exile Editions.

Excerpt from "A Flame on the Spanish Stairs: John Keats in Rome" by Douglas Barbour is used by permission of the poet. "Queen Mary, She's My Friend" taken from *The Spaces In Between* by Stephen Scobie. Reprinted with the permission of NeWest Press. "Constrained Response" by Maxine Berger is used by permission of the poet. "Blōdmōnath" from *anhaga* is used by permission of the estate of Jon Furberg. "Blues" is used by permission of the estate of bp Nichol. "Particle Limericks" from *Animate Objects* is used by permission of Turnstone Press. "Her Other Language" by Nancy Mattson is used by permission of the poet. Excerpt from "Chapter E" from *Eunoia* is used by permission of Coach House Press. "Hand Game" by Frances Boyle is used by permission of the poet.

INDEX OF TERMS

Accent, 227, 283; anapest, 283; dactyl, 283; iamb, 283; trochee, 283

Acrostic, 261

Alexandrine, 207, 286

Alliteration, 261, 289, *see also* Rhyme

Amphibrach, *see* Foot

Amphimacer, *see* Foot

Anadiplosis, 287

Anapest, *see* Foot

Anaphora, 287

Anerca, 276

Anglo-Saxon, 116, 261

Assonance, 289, *see also* Rhyme

Ballad stanza, 21

Ballad, 21-22

Blank verse, 190, 288

Blues, 36-37

Burden, *see* Refrain

Caesura, 261, 281

Call-and-response, 37

Calligramme, *see* Visual poem

Catalectic, *see* Foot

Cinquain, 228, 229

Concrete, *see* Visual poem

Consonance, 289, *see also* Rhyme

Couplet, 49-50, 282; closed, 49; heroic, 49; open, 49; rhymed, 291; short, 49; ghazal, 78

Dactyl, *see* Foot

Dimeter, 286

Dramatic monologue, 278

End-stop, 281

Enjamb, 281

Envelope rhyme, 236

Envoy, 175

Epanalepsis, 287

Epigram, 60

Epistrophe, 287

Epitaph, 60

Epizeuxis, 287

Foot, amphibrach, 284; amphimacer, 284; anapest, 284; catalectic, 284; dactyl, 284; iamb, 284; metrical, 283, 284; pyrrhic, 285; spondee, 285; tag, 285; trochee, 285

Form, 13, 15, 16; closed, 14; open, 14

Free verse, 228, 280, 282

Fugue, 18, 68-70

Ghazal, 16, 18, 78-80, 275

Glosa, 88-89, 163

Haibun, 103, 104

Haiku, 18, 78, 80, 103-105, 189, 228, 236, 275

Heptameter, 286

Heterometric, 281

Hexameter, 286

Hokku, 103

Iamb, *see* Foot

Incantation, 18, 116-117; chants, 116; charms, 116; spells, 116

Incremental repetition, *see* Refrain

Indentation, 281

Isometric, 281-282

Iteratio, 287

Kidai, 103

Kigo, 103

Limerick, 262

Line, 280

Lipogram, 189, 262

List poem, 116

Madrigal, 68-70

Madsong, 262, 274

Matla, 80

Metre, 280, 282-286; accentual, 282; accentual-syllabic, 282; free verse, 282; long, 209; patterns, 283-286; quantitative, 282; syllabic, 282

Monometer, 286

Mukta, 80

Music, 36, 68, 78, 283, 288-289

Nonce, 18, 49

Octameter, 286

Octet, 282

Onji, 103

Onomatopoeia, 290, *see also* Rhyme

Oulipo, 262

INDEX OF POETS

ACKNOWLEDGEMENTS

We are grateful to the numerous people who have helped us during our three year journey with this book. The following generously provided us with their expertise, advice and feedback: Marianne Bluger, Charles Boname, George Elliott Clarke, Harvey DeRoo, Gary Geddes, Alice Korfman, Nadeem Parmar, Robyn Sarah and Tom Wayman. (It is none of their doing if any errors have crept into these pages.) We are also grateful to the librarians in the Canadian poetry section of the Vancouver Public Library for their research assistance.

Thanks also to the original prosody group members who, in delving into theories of form with us, helped to lay the foundations for this book: Julie Archer, Antonia Banyard, Natalie Meisner, Nicola Aime, Susan McRae — and Keith Maillard, who helped the group gain a deeper understanding of metre and the New Formalism. Special thanks go to all the poets writing in form whose work provided a wealth of excellent poems for us to choose from. We particularly appreciate the enthusiasm with which poets across the country greeted this project.

Kate would like to thank the Malaspina University-College Research and Scholarly Activity Committee and the Malaspina Faculty Association, for funds to help in the research for this book. She also thanks the English and Creative Writing & Journalism faculties for their support, especially Keith Harrison who asked her to teach the first course in writing form poetry at Malaspina. That course pushed her into the hot bath she's been splashing happily in ever since.

Sandy thanks the two teachers extraordinaire who first nurtured her enduring love of form — Tom Trafford and Helen Beale; two poets who first introduced her to intriguing new forms — Kirsten Emmott and Gudrun Wight; and every poet who ever wrote a poem that left her breathless.

ABOUT THE EDITORS

KATE BRAID has published three poetry collections: *Covering Rough Ground*, *To This Cedar Fountain*, and *Inward to the Bones: Georgia O'Keeffe's Journey with Emily Carr*, all with Polestar. She has also published numerous essays, two books of non-fiction — *Red Bait! Struggles of a Mine Mill Local*, co-authored with Al King, and *Emily Carr: Rebel Artist* — and has edited *The Fish Come In Dancing: Stories from the West Coast Fishery*. She teaches creative writing at Malaspina University-College in Nanaimo, British Columbia, as well as various "nonce" writing workshops. Her poetry books have won the Pat Lowther and the VanCity Book Prizes and been short-listed for the Dorothy Livesay Poetry Prize, the Pat Lowther Prize and the Milton Acorn People's Poetry Award.

SANDY SHREVE has published three poetry collections: *The Speed of the Wheel is Up to the Potter* (Quarry); *Bewildered Rituals* (Polestar); and *Belonging* (Sono Nis), which was shortlisted for the Milton Acorn People's Poetry Award. She founded Poetry in Transit in British Columbia, and for three years coordinated the project. Sandy also edited *Working for a Living*, a collection of poems and stories by women about their work. She has won the Earle Birney Prize for Poetry and has been shortlisted in the poetry category of the National Magazine Awards. She lives in Vancouver, British Columbia, and is the Communications Officer for the Legal Services Society.